100

THINGS TO DO IN

KANSAS

BEFORE YOU

DIE

Happy 100 Things

collecting!

David

D1240860

Arikaree Breaks

100

THINGS TO DO IN
KANSAS
BEFORE YOU
DIE

• •

ROXIE YONKEY

REEDY PRESS

Library of Congress Control Number: 2021935135

ISBN: 9781681063195

Design by Jill Halpin

Photos by author unless otherwise noted.

Printed in the United States of America
22 23 24 25   5 4 3 2

DEDICATION

For my husband, Eric Yonkey.
Thank you for your never-failing love and support.

Sunflowers north of Goodland

CONTENTS

● ●

Music and Entertainment

Sports and Recreation

Culture and History

● ●

• •

ACKNOWLEDGMENTS

My dad, Gene Lockwood, loved wordplay. He had a dry wit, and I inherited my love of words from him. My mother, Mary Lockwood, journaled prolifically.

Mrs. Compton, my first grade teacher, taught me to speed-read, opening the realm of books. I'm grateful to my high school teachers Kevan Extrum, Dale Feeken, Barbara Ide, and Dr. James Loch, and his wife Jeanne.

Teresa (Aman) Hyler, you left us far too early.

In college, I learned from my boss Chuck Burch and from my colleagues and friends Chris Doyle, Mike Montoro, and Pat and Debbie Scales.

At the *Syracuse Journal*, Charity Horinek and Evelyn Drew pushed Eric and me together, making two halves far better as one whole.

Thank you to my proofreaders Cathy Albert and Marilyn Hefner. My tourism journey would not have been as much fun without Cathy. Marilyn drags me out of my writer's cocoon when I need it.

The encouragement and advice of my fellow travel writers Sara Broers, Jody Halsted, Amy Piper, Melody Pittman, and Tim and Lisa Trudell are priceless.

My Marys, Mary Arlington and Mary Ellen Coumerilh, help me combine dreams with reality.

Thanks, Donna Price, for recruiting me into Kansas tourism. A big thank you goes to every destination marketing organization who helped with this book. So often, your work goes unnoticed, but I am grateful.

Lastly, to my family: Eric; Kevin and Stefaney Lockwood, Abbie and Blayde Clark, Alex and Avery Lockwood, Deanna Lockwood, Merlyn and Ruth Anne Yonkey, Eleanor and the late Norman Avery, Gary and Miriam Yonkey, all my cousins, and my best friend Debbie (Amsbaugh) Phillips: you are my inspiration and the wind beneath my wings.

Thank you.

● ●

PREFACE

Kansas is subtle. The Sunflower State doesn't overwhelm visitors with its mountains or its oceans. We have neither. Instead, Kansas sneaks up on its guests, and, before they realize it, they've fallen in love with the state, its friendly people, fascinating history, beauty, and fun activities.

I know this because it happened to me. I've lived in and written about Kansas for over 30 years, and I intended to stay only a year. Marrying the handsome Kansan at the next desk had a lot to do with the 30-year stay, but I was in love with the state before I fell in love with him.

Because I love this state, choosing only 100 things to do in Kansas was a daunting task. (I snuck in as many additional attractions as I could in the tips and venue lists.)

Kansans reach for the stars. The action is enshrined in the state motto: *ad astra per aspera*, to the stars through difficulties. The sculpture *Ad Astra* shoots for the stars from atop the state capitol's dome. Struggling to pick which places would receive a 100 Things nod seems appropriate.

Even though all of the state's 105 counties are worth exploring, I had to consider the state as a whole. What pieces could compose an overall Kansas mosaic? The 100 Things needed icons like Dwight Eisenhower, John Brown, and Amelia Earhart; the big-name museums like the Cosmosphere

• •

in Hutchinson; industry themes like agriculture, aviation, and mining. Yes, mining: Hutchinson's Strataca takes you into a salt mine. Big Brutus mined coal in West Mineral.

The infamous tornadoes also appear.

The 100 Things needed big-city representation and small-town attractions. And they needed to come from the state's corners like the Point of Rocks in Elkhart, the Arikaree Breaks north of St. Francis, and Route 66 at Baxter Springs.

Kansas is all about the outdoors. Before you paddle down the Kansas River, catch a big fish at Milford Reservoir. Grind gravel at the Garmin Gravel Unbound. Pedal your mountain bike on the epic-rated Switchgrass Bike Trail. The Syracuse Sand Dunes are calling your name.

Shop at the Legends in Kansas City and Old Town Wichita. Hunt for treasures in Winfield's antique stores, but explore smaller venues as well. Find everything Kansas at Kansas Originals. The lavender smells divine at Prairie Lavender Farm; spread the scent in your home.

Keep track of your explorations by asking attractions staff to initial the attraction and date your visit. If no one is available to initial your book, just note the date. On social media, show your friends and followers where you've been by using the hashtag #100thingsks.

Learn more about the Sunflower State at @RoxieontheRoad on Facebook, Instagram, LinkedIn, and Twitter.

Let's explore Kansas!

• •

Drinks at the Elephant Bistro, Hoxie

VARIATIONS ON THE
MANHATTAN

LITTLE APPLE'S BEE $10.00
Drambuie Isle of Skye Scoth Liqueur,
Noilly Prat Dry Vermouth, Angostura Bitters

HELL'S KITCHEN $8.00
Bushmills Irish Whiskey,
Dolin's Vermouth Rouge, Angostura Bitters

THE ROOSTER $12.00
Hennessy Cognac, Dolin's Vermouth
Rouge, Woodford Reserve Sassafras
& Sorghum Bitters

BLACK DIAMOND $10.00
Bushmills Irish Whiskey, Averna,
Angostura bitters, housemade orange bitters,
fresh thyme and a twist of orange

DRINKS TO
KEEP YOU WARM

CAFÉ PUCCI

FOOD AND DRINK

REACH YOUR IMPOSSIBLE DREAM
WITH A TASTE OF AD ASTRA

Kansans have survived a civil war, insect plagues, the Dust Bowl, the Great Depression, and other calamities. And Kansans persist. Because of their struggles, they love their state motto, *ad astra per aspera*, Latin for "to the stars through difficulties." The phrase's coiner explained that Kansas aspires "to reach the unattainable; its dream is the realization of the impossible."

Kansans shorten the motto to *ad astra*.

Celebrate your impossible dream by drinking Ad Astra Ale with Ad Astra Crab Cakes and a Bad Astra French Dip at Ad Astra Food and Drink. The café sits on the Flint Hills Scenic Byway in Strong City. Perch at the bar or sit at the tables. As you eat, examine the Kansas-themed décor.

318 Cottonwood St., Strong City, KS 66869, (620) 273-8840
adastrafoodanddrink.com

TIP

In June, watch Strong City's Flint Hills Rodeo,
Kansas's oldest continuously operating rodeo.

Strong City Rodeo Grounds, 300 E. Seventh St., Strong City, KS 66869
flinthillsrodeo.org

TANTALIZE YOUR TONGUE
ON THE KCK TACO TRAIL

Simply reading the taco descriptions on the Kansas City, Kansas, (KCK) "Taco Trail 101" page tantalizes your tongue—and your other senses. Let these words roll off your tongue: adobada, carnitas, chorizo, jamon, longaniza, nopal, pollo . . . . Hear sizzling carne asada on the grill. Watch the taquero cut al pastor meat from the trompo.

Are you hungry yet? You'll need to be. KCK lists more than 50 places to savor tacos. Many are small and immigrant-owned. When you smell the aroma of chicharrón, you'll know you've arrived.

Some restaurants offer authentic Mexican styles. Some offer Tex-Mex, and some, like El Torito Supermart, offer vegetarian tacos. Savor taco styles from northern Mexico at Carniceria y Tortilleria San Antonio and Veracruz-style fish tacos at Jarocho Pescados y Mariscos.

visitkansascityks.com/blog/post/kck-taco-trail-101

TIP

Create your own taco recipes with Spicin Foods spice blends.

111 Southwest Blvd., Kansas City, KS 66103, (913) 432-5228
spicinfoods.com

STRUT WITH SOME BARBECUE
IN KANSAS CITY

Barbecue laced with sweet and tangy sauce is Kansas City's gift to American cuisine. Thick Kansas City-style sauce includes tomato, molasses, and sometimes brown sugar. Pitmasters may infuse the sauce into the meat while cooking or slather it on afterward.

While KC pitmasters use every meat, burnt ends define the barbecue style. Burnt ends are the point of the brisket muscle, the deckle. The finished brisket releases flavor explosions in your mouth.

SLAP's BBQ sells out nearly daily. Come on Tuesdays for delicious Burnt End Tacos.

Joe's Kansas City Bar-B-Que's building was once a gas station. Fill your stomach with ribs served with red beans and rice.

At Woodyard Bar-B-Que, the aroma of white oak and hickory wafting from their outdoor smoker only enhances the flavor waiting inside.

visitkansascityks.com/restaurants/barbeque

TIP

John LeRoy Marshall designed the Rosedale Arch after the Arc de Triomphe in Paris. The arch and the monument below it honor neighborhood veterans.

35th and Booth St., Kansas City, KS 66103, (913) 573-8327
visitkansascityks.com/listing/rosedale-memorial-arch/74

SINK YOUR TEETH
INTO A STRAWBERRY HILL POVITICA

A povitica is a Croatian pastry, pronounced "po-va-TEET-sa." Call it a povi for short. Strawberry Hill Bakery's recipe is authentic, handed down through generations.

While a povi is a pastry, the handmade dough's texture is more like cake batter. The pastry chef rolls the dough until it's thin enough to read a newspaper while looking through it. Then the chef rolls the dough around the filling. Finally, the chef folds the povi into an "S" shape and bakes it.

Povis aren't among the pastries that include more dough than filling. Instead, the baker stuffs them with three times more filling than the dough that contains it.

Pick from 13 different flavors, including cranberry walnut, cokolada (chocolate), strawberry cream cheese, and lemon blueberry cream cheese.

7226 W. Frontage Rd., Merriam, KS 66203, (800) 631-1002
strawberryhill.com

TIP
At the Strawberry Hill Museum & Cultural Center, learn about Kansas City's ethnicities, and eat dessert in the tearoom.

720 N. Fourth St., Kansas City, KS 66101, (913) 371-3264
strawberryhillmuseum.org

SQUEAK YOUR WAY TO CHEESE CURD PARADISE
AT ALMA CREAMERY

Reach into a bag of Alma Creamery's cheese curds and raise one to your mouth. Bite down for an instant freshness check. Fresh cheese curds squeak. When you hear the squeaky cheese, you know you've just eaten Kansas's best "nibblin' good" cheese. Why does the cheese squeak? Developing protein chains are rubbing against your tooth enamel.

The creamery's signature product is the ultimate road-tripping snack. Curds are available from outlets throughout the state. Visit the creamery for the best way to experience Alma Cheese, where you'll see local milk turned into delicious handmade jack and cheddar cheese. Try free samples before making your final decision. The store also sells their summer sausage, plus other Kansas food vendors' products.

For a delightful gift, purchase a gift box.

509 E. Third St., Alma, KS 66401, (785) 765-3522
almacheese.com

TIP
Shop at Grandma Hoerner's Natural and Organic Foods outlet. Take I-70 Exit 324, the next exit west of Alma Creamery's exit.

31862 Thompson Rd., Alma, KS 66401, (785) 765-2300
grandmahoerners.com

FIND HEAVEN ON TOP OF AN ICE CREAM CONE
AT CALL HALL DAIRY BAR

Every day, Call Hall Dairy Bar at Kansas State University stocks 16 different ice cream flavors in its dipping cabinets. Luscious flavors include After Dinner Mint, Apple Dapple, Chocolate Brownie Delight, Purple Pride, Swiss Chocolate Almond, and Wild Thing. Lick them off a cone or choose containers. Pair the ice cream with sandwiches.

Call Hall is the ultimate "farm-to-spoon" facility. From breeding K-State's dairy cattle to raw milk processing, every dairy production stage occurs within two miles of the retail outlets.

The stores' products aren't limited to ice cream. Choose from milk, 11 cheese varieties, and five different cheese spreads. K-State poultry sells free-range hormone- and antibiotic-free eggs. Buy lamb, beef, pork, and poultry from K-State's meat labs. Smoked hams, turkeys, and processed meat products are seasonally available.

1530 N. Mid-Campus Dr., Manhattan, KS 66506, (785) 532-1292
asi.k-state.edu/about/services-and-sales/call-hall-dairy-bar.html

---

TIP
Call Hall at the Union offers ice cream-related products only.

142 Kansas State Student Union, 918 N. 17th St., (785) 532-1302

ARRIVE EARLY AND STAY LATE

IN AGGIEVILLE

Aggieville is the oldest shopping district in Kansas, but we love it as a place to eat, drink, and hang out. More than 50 restaurants and bars open their doors in Aggieville. While the district is Kansas's oldest, the vibe skews young. Aggieville is Kansas State University's next-door neighbor.

Start the morning at Varsity Donuts with bins full of yummy options. For lunch, devour a Portobello quesadilla and a stacked enchilada at Taco Lucha. End the day with cocktails and pizza at the Hi-Lo.

In between meals, browse the retailers. Check out the Sisters of Sound music store and the Dusty Bookshelf bookstore.

On K-State game days, hang out at Johnny Kaw's Sports Bar to paint Manhattan purple. Buy Wildcat apparel at Rally House.

aggieville.org

TIP

Johnny Kaw's statue stands in Johnny Kaw Plaza, part of Manhattan's City Park. Kansas's answer to Paul Bunyan is the optimal selfie subject.

1220 Poyntz Ave., mhkprd.com/285/Johnny-Kaw-Statue

DINE WITH THE DYNASTY
IN THE FRIED CHICKEN CAPITAL OF KANSAS

A mining accident started the Crawford County's fried chicken restaurant dynasty in 1934. The delicious chicken continues to draw crowds.

Ann Pichler started the Pittsburg fried-chicken tradition after a mine accident crippled her husband Charlie. Chicken Annie's Original began in 1934 in the Pichlers' home, serving chicken, potato salad, coleslaw, a pickled pepper strip, and a tomato slice on bread.

Poor health ruined Joe Zerngast's mining career in the 1940s. Mary Zerngast began serving fried chicken at home, including potato salad and coleslaw. By 1945, the Zerngasts had established Chicken Mary's. The two restaurants are nearly side by side.

Louis and Louella (Pichler) Lipoglav started Chicken Annie's Girard in 1971. The Girard restaurant fries its chicken to order.

Eventually, the original Pichlers' grandson Anthony Pichler married the Zerngasts' granddaughter Donna Zerngast. The couple opened Pichler's Chicken Annie's.

All of the restaurants serve bread from the Frontenac Bakery.

visitcrawfordcounty.com/front/friedchicken

ENTER FRIED CHICKEN HEAVEN

Eat the divine at Crawford County's
six fried-chicken restaurants.

Barto's Idle Hour
201 Santa Fe St., Frontenac, KS 66763
(620) 232-9834, bartosidlehour.com

Chicken Annie's Girard
498 E. Hwy. 47, Girard, KS, 66743
(620) 724-4090, chickenanniesgirard.com

Chicken Annie's Orginal
1143 E. 600th Ave., Pittsburg, KS 66762
(620) 231-9460, chickenanniesoriginal.com

Chicken Mary's
1133 E. 600th Ave., Pittsburg, KS 66762
(620) 231-9510, chicken-marys.com

Frontenac Bakery
211 N. Crawford, Frontenac, KS 66763,
(785) 231-7980, facebook.com/FrontenacBakery

Gebhardt's
124 N. 260th St., Mulberry, KS 66756
(620) 764-3451

Pichler's Chicken Annie's
1271 S. 220th St., Pittsburg, KS 66762
(620) 232-9260, facebook.com/Pichlers-
Chicken-Annies-126714840749192/

TASTE ITALY
AT JOSIE'S RISTORANTE

When you go to Josie's Ristorante, expect to wait. And expect the wait to be worth your time.

Frank and Josie Saporito emigrated from Italy in 1904. He was seeking a mining career. She brought Italian family recipes. The Saporitos' grandson Mike and his wife Sally opened their restaurant in 1986 in an 1890s grocery store. The restaurant's staff prepares the sauce and pasta daily.

All the menu options are delicious, but the chicken Parmesan, lasagna, fried ravioli, and spaghetti are exceptional. Save room for the Italian cream cake.

Capture some of the magic by bringing home a jar of Josie's sauce. Are you wondering what to serve at your next gathering? Feed them all with an entire pan of pasta. Bring cash, because the restaurant doesn't accept credit cards.

400 N. Main St., Scammon, KS 66773, (620) 479-8202
facebook.com/josiesristorante

TIP
Ride the train at the Heart of the
Heartlands Museum Complex, three miles east of Josie's.
6769 NW 20th St., (620) 423-5163, heartlandstrainclub.org

DARE TO DEVOUR THE NUTS
AT PRAIRIE NUT HUT

The nuts at Prairie Nut Hut do not grow on trees, nor can they be found underground. Instead of vegetation, they are the fruit of a male animal. That's right; they're testicles. Prairie Nut Hut has a ball with its bull fries. Its logo's bull brags, "Ha, ha! I've still got mine."

The Nut Hut is the epitome of a rural bar. It seats 40, which includes all the barstools. Peanut shells litter the floor, the walls sparkle with Christmas lights, and photos of visitors from around the world paper the walls.

Of course, the mountain oysters aren't the sole menu item. Try the generously-portioned burgers. We recommend the Rohr Burger with grilled onions, mushrooms, and Swiss cheese. Don't leave without a souvenir T-shirt.

1306 Quincy St., Altoona, KS 66710, (620) 568-2900
kansassampler.org/8wondersofkansas-cuisine/prairie-nut-hut-altoona

---

TIP
Safari with Martin and Osa Johnson
at their namesake museum 15 miles away in Chanute.

111 N. Lincoln, Chanute, KS 66720, (620) 431-2730, safarimuseum.com

---

BINGE ON
A BAG OF BURGERS
AT THE COZY INN

To find the Cozy Inn in downtown Salina, step outside and follow your nose. The smell of burgers frying and onions will lead you unerringly to Cozy Inn's door. The menu is simple: palm-sized fresh-made ground-beef sliders with raw onions. No cheese. Nothing at the Cozy is frozen. And business is good. The staff grills thousands of little burgers daily. Like the sign says: buy them by the sack!

Cozy's founder, Bob Kinkel, borrowed the slider idea from White Castle in 1922. The palm-sized burgers got the "slider" name because cooks slid them to customers on waxed paper.

Protect your clothes; keep the bag of burgers away from fabric. If you don't want to smell onion burgers for days, don't let the burgers sit in your car either.

108 N. Seventh St., Salina, KS 67401, (785) 825-2699
cozyburger.com

TIP
Finish your meal with a treat at Dagney's Ice Cream.
For the best service, order ahead.

105 E. Iron Ave., (785) 833-2125, dagneysicecream.com

TRANSCEND TIME AND SPACE
AT C. W. PORUBSKY'S DELI & TAVERN

Your map app may not find Porubsky's immediately. And when you arrive, the sign says nothing about a restaurant. Instead, it reads "Porubsky Groc."

Don't let the sign mislead you. A 30-seat tavern is hiding inside the store.

When you walk in, you'll feel as if you've entered another time. The food is a throwback, too, but who cares? Modern is overrated compared to Porubsky's.

Porubsky's is most famous for its chili, but they only sell it from Labor Day until the end of April. If it's not chili season, order the deli sandwiches. If you appreciate horseradish, try the horseradish pickles. Take home some pimento spread, but be warned: the hot condiment version is scorching, and the effect is cumulative.

Porubsky's does not accept credit cards.

508 NE Sardou Ave., Topeka, KS 66608, (785) 234-5788
facebook.com/pages/CW-Porubsky-Grocery-and-Meats/131331040244774

TIP
Check out the gourmet grilled cheese sandwiches
at The Wheel Barrel a few blocks northwest of Porubsky's.

925 N. Kansas Ave., (785) 289-6767, thewheelbarrel.com

SNEAK AWAY TO A VINTAGE ROADHOUSE
AT NORTH STAR STEAKHOUSE

You have to want to eat at Topeka's North Star Steakhouse. It's isolated like a Prohibition-era roadhouse—for a good reason. You'll think, "Am I going to witness a murder?"

North Star founder William E. "Jug" Robinson was a bootlegger. Topeka law enforcement never caught him, but Kansas City did. Robinson's picture still hangs at the bar.

Robinson's reputation aside, your first bite of steak will bring you back to the Star every time you visit Topeka. Those who are desperately hungry can try the 32-ounce porterhouse steak. If that's a stretch, split the Steak for Two, 32 ounces of sirloin. The bacon-wrapped filet is just right for one.

Express your Prohibition opinion with the Star's Prohibition-era cocktails. The North Side is our favorite.

1100 NW 25th St., Topeka, KS 66618, (785) 354-8880
northstarsteakhouse.com

TIP
The restaurant doesn't require reservations, but they recommend them. Reserve online, or call ahead for same-day reservations.

BEEF UP YOUR MEAL IN KANSAS STEAKHOUSES

Big Ed's Steakhouse
106 W. Bressler, Bird City, KS 67731
(785) 734-2475, facebook.com/Big-Eds-
Steakhouse-Bird-City-102467704448574

Crazy R's Bar & Grill
1618 Main St., Goodland, KS 67735
(785) 890-3430, facebook.com/
CrazyRsBarAndGrill

Grand Central Hotel & Grill
215 Broadway, Cottonwood Falls, KS 66845
(620) 273-6763, grandcentralhotel.com

Scotch and Sirloin
5325 E. Kellogg Dr., Wichita, KS 67218
(316) 685-8701, scotchandsirloin.net

Town's End Tavern
117 N. Main St., Sharon Springs, KS 67758
(719) 342-1359, facebook.com/townsendtav

FEAST ON THE EXTRAORDINARY
AT THE ELEPHANT BISTRO & BAR

The Elephant Bistro and Bar's founder and executive chef Emily Campbell set out to provide "something out of the ordinary." She has succeeded. The Elephant's exterior is stunning. Campbell converted a former storefront into a beautiful oasis. The interior and the menu fulfill her extraordinary vision.

The Elephant uses locally sourced ingredients whenever possible. French cooking techniques meet multicultural cuisine elements while protecting the environment.

The Campbells built the restaurant's furniture with wood salvaged from the building's second floor. They made the bar from the former Hoxie bowling alley's lanes.

We recommend the Italian pork chop agrodolce and creamy Chantilly potatoes. Finish your meal with Mt. Rainier s'mores, served on a cedar plank and flambéed at your table.

The restaurant recommends reservations.

732 Main St., Hoxie, KS 67740, (785) 677-3977
theelephantbistrobar.com

TIP

Step into ranching history
at Cottonwood Ranch State Historic
Site east of Hoxie.

14432 E. Hwy. 24, Studley, KS 67759
(785) 627-5866, kshs.org/p/
cottonwood-ranch/19571

DREAM OF CULINARY DELIGHTS
AT DESTINATION KITCHEN

No surprise: Destination Kitchen is about selling food. But the store addresses both the front and the back of the house. Destination Kitchen is both a high-end kitchen store and a wood-fired pizzeria, deli, and bakery.

The store stocks brands like All-Clad, Cuisinart, and KitchenAid. They also sell upscale food preparation tools and gourmet ingredients. Order your pizza or sandwich first, then browse the retail section.

Browsing inspires you to improve your kitchen skills with quality tools.

Between the aisles, watch pizza baking in the brick oven. The aroma permeates the store. Eat your meal while sipping a lemonade. As you gaze around the store, relax and dream of your kitchen successes to come. Finish your meal with a tasty pastry.

115 W. Main St., Norton, KS 67654, (785) 877-2911

destinationkitchenks.com

TIP
A door on Destination's south side
opens into Stitch Up a Storm, a fabric store.

113 W. Main St., Norton, KS 67654, (785) 874-5152
facebook.com/Stitch-Up-A-Storm-222167207799520

PARTAKE IN HISTORY
AT THE HAYS HOUSE

Daniel Boone's great-grandson, Seth Hays, arrived in Council Grove in 1847. He opened a store and eatery on the Santa Fe Trail. Ten years later, he built Hays House next to the trail. It's the oldest continuously operating restaurant west of the Mississippi River.

Order the Wabaunsee Wrangler sandwich or the bacon and cheddar meatloaf with a side of HH fries.

After you order, roam through the building. In the cellar bar, it's easy to imagine Santa Fe Trail teamsters drinking after a hard day driving their teams. Examine the crystal room's collection on the second floor. Ask to see the handbag collection.

The historic building also served as a courtroom, post office, and performance venue. On Saturday nights, the staff covered the liquor bottles to prepare for church on Sunday mornings.

112 W. Main St., Council Grove, KS 66846, (620) 767-5911
hayshouse.com

TIP
Walk off your meal on the Pioneer Nature Trail.
945 Lake Rd., (620) 767-5195,
americantrails.org/resources/pioneer-nature-trail-kansas

INDULGE YOUR SWEET TOOTH
WITH MARCON PIES

Marilyn Hanshaw and Connie Allen decided to bake pies in their hometown, Washington. They combined their first names and called their company MarCon Pies. Their delicious pies quickly gained a following. Soon, they outgrew their homes and had to open a bakery. The orders rolled in from all over the region.

In 2018, MarCon closed, to pie lovers' dismay. But the company was back in business in 2020 when Craig and Mary Ann Stertz moved the bakery from Washington to Lincoln.

MarCon crafts their nine-inch fruit, creme, crunch, specialty, and no-sugar-added pies daily, using heirloom recipes and quality ingredients. They mix fillings and crimp tender, flaky crusts by hand. They bake more than 80 pie varieties, but apple and cherry are their bestsellers.

114 W. Lincoln Ave., Lincoln, KS 67455, (785) 524-2264
marconpies.com

TIP
MarCon is a wholesaler that sells to vendors within 120 miles of Lincoln. Find their vendors at marconpies.com/become-a-vendor.

VENERATE THE KANSAS PIE PANTHEON

From sky-high meringue to delectable fillings,
every day is Pie Day at these restaurants.

Aunt Netter's Café
336 Elmore St., Lecompton, KS 66050
(785) 503-6004, auntnetters.com

Betty's Pies & Cobblers
648 205 W. Main, Gardner, KS 66030
(913) 221-4592, bettyspiesandcobblers.com

Carriage Crossing Restaurant and Bakery
10002 S. Yoder Rd., Yoder, KS 67585
(620) 465-3612, yoderkansas.com/carriagecrossing

Don's Place
220 N. Broadway Ave., Protection, KS 67127
(620) 622-4365, facebook.com/donsplaceprotectionkansas

Made from Scratch
The World's Largest Czech Egg is down the street.
527 27th St., Wilson, KS 67490
(785) 658-3300, facebook.com/Made-From-
Scratch-102742546467467

Rye Leawood
10551 Mission Rd., Leawood, KS 66206
(913) 642-5800, ryekc.com

Sommerset Café
5701 SW Douglas Rd., Dover, KS 66610
(785) 256-6223, facebook.com/Sommerset-
Cafe-106870290828068

Spear's Restaurant and Pie Shop
4323 W. Maple St., Wichita, KS 67209
(316) 943-2783, spearsrestaurant.com

The Upper Crust
7943 Santa Fe Dr., Overland Park, KS 66204
(913) 642-2999, uppercrustpiebakery.com

REFINE YOUR TASTE IN WINES
AT JENNY DAWN CELLARS

Tasting notes from Jenny Dawn Cellars could include many descriptors. All of her wines are smooth from the first sip to the final one. You'll taste no bitter brutality on your tongue when you drain the bottle's last drop. As a bonus, savor delicious small bites with your wine tasting.

Wine and wine-making fascinated Jennifer McDonald from an early age. She resolved to become a winemaker. A pioneer, she's the first African-American commercial winemaker in Kansas and owns Wichita's first urban winery.

McDonald's minimalist tasting room reflects her wines. Everything is sleek and carefully arranged. Splashes of the winery's signature color, purple, are everywhere. The warmth counteracts the cool metal, creating a relaxing vibe. Plenty of awards enliven the decor.

703 E. Douglas Ave., Ste. 180, Wichita, KS 67202, (316) 633-3022
jennydawncellars.com

TIP
Every third Tuesday, Jenny Dawn holds "wineucation" sessions. Guests try six wines from around the world, paired with three appetizers.

SCOOT YOUR BOOTS BELOW THE BAR
AT BOOT HILL DISTILLERY

Dodge City's Boot Hill Distillery stands on the Boot Hill Cemetery lot. Nearly a century ago, the city disinterred and moved all the bodies. So don't worry—you won't disrespect anyone by visiting the tasting room.

The distillery controls its product from "soil to sip." They grow and distill the grain.

Boot Hill's tasting room feels like a cocktail lounge with a copper-topped bar, a vintage cash register, and Edison lights. Sit at the leather-topped iron barstools, in the stuffed leather sofas and lounge chairs, or at a table. Let the stress fade away while you sip a cocktail. Try the Rosemary Mule, the Liquid S'Mores, and the Buttered Bourbon.

Don't leave without a bottle of whiskey or some of their premade cocktails.

501 W. Spruce St., Dodge City, KS 67801, (620) 371-6309
boothilldistillery.com

TIP
For more delicious Kansas spirits, visit Union Horse Distilling Co.
11740 W. 86th Terr., Lenexa, KS 66214,
(913) 492-3275, unionhorse.com

QUAFF LIQUID BREAD
AT GELLA'S DINER AND LB. BREWING

We'll always remember the first time we walked into Gella's Diner and Lb. Brewing Co. (Lb. stands for "liquid bread.") The building and furnishings were industrial, which often translates into coldness: but not at Gella's. The recreated vintage advertising signs and wooden tabletops made the ample space feel cozy and welcoming.

We were craft beer newbies and knew nothing about selecting brews. The wait staff patiently guided us to pick beers to our tastes. We were impressed.

Since that day, we've tried numerous craft beers all over the United States. Gella's still stands up to the competition. We also love the beef stroganoff, bierocks, and creamed spinach. The beers rotate, so you'll always have something new to try. We favor the American hefeweizen and raspberry wheat beers when available.

117 E. 11th St., Hays, KS 67601, (785) 621-BREW
lbbrewing.com

TIP

Try more local beer at Defiance Brewing Co.

2050 E. Hwy. 40, Hays, KS 67601, (785) 301-BEER
defiancebeer.com

RAISE YOUR GLASS TO KANSAS CRAFT BREWS

Blue Skye Brewery & Eats
116 N. Santa Fe, Salina, KS 67401
(785) 404-2159, facebook.com/blueskyebrewery

Kansas Territory Brewing Company
310 C St., Washington, KS 66968
(785) 325-3300, kansasterritorybrewingco.com/contact.html

Manhattan Brewing Company
406 Poyntz Ave., Manhattan, KS 66502
(785) 775-0406, mhkbeer.com

Nortons Brewing Co.
125 St. Francis St., Wichita, KS 67202
(316) 425-9009, nortonsbrewing.com

Tallgrass Tap House
320 Poyntz Ave., Manhattan, KS 66502
(785) 320-2933, tallgrasstaphouse.com

Walnut River Brewing Co.
111 W. Locust Ave., El Dorado, KS 67042
(316) 351-8086, walnutriverbrewing.com

Wichita Brewing Company & Pizzeria
8815 W. 13th St., Suite 100, Wichita, KS 67212
(316) 440-2885, wichitabrew.com

SIP DELICIOUS CIDER
AT LOUISBURG CIDER MILL

You pour Louisburg Cider into a cold glass and raise it to your lips. You sip the fruit of 1,000-pound bins of Jonathan, Red Delicious, and Golden Delicious apples from Kansas and Missouri orchards. As you continue drinking, visions of Kansas's fall delights swirl through your mind.

After you finish drinking the glass, you decide to visit the cider mill. You join a tour. Lovely aromas surround you as you observe apples crushed into cider. You choose an apple-cider donut, then eat another and another. As you lick your fingers to capture every last morsel, you solve the corn maze and wander through the pumpkin patch. At the country store, you buy some Lost Trail Root Beer and cherry butter.

You go home happy.

14730 Hwy. 68, Louisburg, KS 66053, (913) 837-5202
louisburgcidermill.com

TIP
Learn about big cats at Louisburg's Cedar Cove Feline Conservation Park.
3783 Hwy. 68, (913) 837-5515, saveoursiberians.org

IMPROVE YOUR BAKING
WITH HEARTLAND MILL

Bread recipes start with simple ingredients: flour, water, yeast, and salt. The ingredients' quality and the baker's skill determine the results.

The best flour comes from the best grain. Heartland Mill sources the best organic grain and grinds the best flour.

Their strong bread flour is excellent for pizza crust, rye, and sourdough. Baker's patent flour improves pastries. Use Golden Buffalo and all-purpose flour for French bread, and whole wheat flour for cookies and quick bread. Combine steel-cut oats with whole wheat for top-notch oatmeal cookies. Heartland's fluffy, bright-yellow cornmeal is superior to anything found in grocery stores.

Buy Heartland Mill's baked goods at The Country Oven, their bakery next door. Order a cake for your next special occasion.

124 N. Hwy. 167, Marienthal, KS 67863, (620) 379-4472
heartlandmill.com

TIP
Shop at Hoffman Grist Mill's store in Enterprise, a stop on the Abilene & Smoky Valley Railroad. Board the ASVRR at 200 SE Fifth Street, Abilene, KS 67410, (785) 263-1077, asvrr.org.

SPICE UP YOUR LIFE
WITH OLDE WESTPORT SPICE

If you're lucky, you'll walk into Goodland's Olde Westport Spice on blending day. The aromas that pour out of the factory inspire you to create in your kitchen.

Bill Petersen, "Olde Bill," experimented with dry spice blends to improve his cooking. Then he started selling them.

Petersen has won numerous chili contests with his championship chili blend. At trade shows, the Olde Westport booth draws attention from the chili aroma alone. When people sample the dish, they buy the spice blend. You should, too. We use his beef sauce extensively in beef dishes.

Unsure how to use the spice blends? Buy a Westport cookbook.

Westport also makes delicious dry soup blends. Our favorites are the red beans and rice and the Southwestern corn tortilla soup.

1218 Main St., Goodland, KS 67735, (785) 899-2020
oldewestportspice.com

TIP

Sample the blends at the family's restaurant, Westport on Main, in front of the spice factory. After dinner, hang out at Terra Bona Hawai'ian Shaved Ice & Coffee Company next door, then watch a movie across the street at the Sherman Theatre.

the1200block.com

INSPIRE YOUR INNER ENTREPRENEUR
AT THE PIZZA HUT MUSEUM

In 1958, Dan and Frank Carney opened a tiny pizza parlor near the Wichita State University campus, where they were students. The sign only had room for nine letters. "Pizza" required five, and a space between words left room for only three more letters. They chose "Hut." On opening night, the kitchen caught fire, and the Carneys had to close temporarily.

In the *ad astra* spirit, they persevered and prevailed.

Pizza Hut has spread worldwide from its inauspicious start, with more than 11,000 restaurants in 90 countries.

WSU moved Pizza Hut's original building to campus in 1986 as a museum. Exhibits include the magazine article that inspired the brothers to serve pizza, a Tiffany-style Pizza Hut light fixture, and Pizza Hut basketball shoes.

The lesson: reach for the stars, even through difficulties.

2090 Innovation Blvd., Wichita, KS 67208, (316) 978-4488
wichita.edu/museums/pizzahutmuseum

TIP
The museum's closest Pizza Hut is at 2129 N. Woodlawn Street, but Wichita has many more of the chain's outlets.

APPLAUD NATURE
AT THE NATIONAL AGRICULTURAL CENTER AND HALL OF FAME

Food starts with farmers. As the nation becomes more urbanized, agriculture's importance is less understood. Agriculture is the state of Kansas's largest industry, and we lead the country in winter wheat production. While one of the state's nicknames is the Wheat State, even many Kansans are ignorant about farming.

At the National Agricultural Center and Hall of Fame, you can learn where food begins its journey to your table, watch farm technology evolve, and "meet" the people who advanced agriculture.

What can people do at the Ag Center? Sit spellbound while farmers spin tales. Uncover the secrets buried within the soil. Dive deep into regional recipes and hear their stories. Learn how vegetables have changed over time. Engage farm animals. Join the fun at seasonal Bee Boot Camp and Chick Days.

630 N. 126th St., Bonner Springs, KS 66012, (913) 721-1075
aghalloffame.com

TIP
Visit the Ag Center in October to watch over 5,000 utility linemen from all over the world compete in the International Lineman's Rodeo.

aghalloffame.com/international-linemans-rodeo

The Stiefel Theatre, Salina

MUSIC AND ENTERTAINMENT

SING
"HOME ON THE RANGE"
AT THE "HOME ON THE RANGE" CABIN

Dr. Brewster Higley needed a change of scenery, and he settled along Beaver Creek in Smith County in the 1870s.

One day, Higley wrote a poem, "My Western Home." The poem would become "Home on the Range," the official Kansas state song.

When Trube Reese read the poem, he suggested that Dan Kelley set it to music. The song became an instant hit for Kelley's orchestra.

Eventually, the song spread throughout the West, but Higley's authorship was lost.

In 1905, a couple from Arizona filed a copyright suit for "My Arizona Home." Their claim sparked an investigation into the song's authorship. The investigator found Reese and Cal Harlan, members of Kelley's orchestra. They explained the song's true origins.

Higley's cabin still stands 10 miles northwest of Athol (pronounced AY-thole).

7032 90 Rd., Athol, KS 66932, (785) 476-5216
homeontherangecabin.com

TIP
"Home on the Range" is ninth on
the Western Writers of America's Top 100 Western Songs.

SURRENDER TO THE SUBLIME
AT THE SYMPHONY IN THE FLINT HILLS

At sunset, the Kansas City Symphony streams sublime sounds through the skies over the Flint Hills. The audience stands as the orchestra begins to play "Home on the Range." They sway and sing to the music.

The stars blaze as the sun disappears. After the concert ends, people remain to gaze at the star-strewn sky. Another triumphant Symphony in the Flint Hills Signature Event ends with delight.

Every year, the event takes place in a different Flint Hills pasture. Spend the afternoon exploring, visiting the vendors, listening to poetry, and riding in a covered wagon.

Bring your water bottle. Pack out everything you bring in. Wear closed-toe walking shoes. Hay wagon rides are available. The event accommodates persons with disabilities whenever possible.

331 Broadway St., Cottonwood Falls, KS 66845, (620) 273-8955

symphonyintheflinthills.org

TIP

Classical music fans will embrace Chamber Music at the Barn.

Prairie Pines, 4055 N. Tyler Rd., Maize, KS 67101

(316) 721-7666, cmatb.org

JAM TO THE MUSIC
AT EMMA CHASE FRIDAY NIGHT MUSIC

On selected Friday nights, musicians and music lovers gather in Cottonwood Falls for Emma Chase Friday Night Music. It's an all-evening jam session. Stay all evening or come and go. Each musician leads a song while others play along. All ability levels are welcome to play, and each night features a specific genre.

Most of the year, the musicians play at Prairie PastTimes, 220 1/2 Broadway. The venue provides seating.

During warm weather, the event moves outdoors, in front of the Symphony in the Flint Hills building, 331 Broadway. The City of Cottonwood Falls reserves portions of Main Street for audience seating. Bring a lawn chair.

Check Facebook.com/EmmaChaseMusic for updates, and watch for street signs.

chasecountychamber.org/emma-chase-friday-night-music
facebook.com/EmmaChaseMusic

TIP

Tour the Chase County Courthouse, a Second Empire-style masterpiece on the south end of Broadway, during business hours.

300 Pearl St., Cottonwood Falls, KS 66845, (620) 273-8469
cwfks.org/chase-county-courthouse

LISTEN TO CHAMPIONSHIP MUSICIANS
AT THE WALNUT VALLEY FESTIVAL

Hear the best acoustic music at Winfield's Walnut Valley Festival during the third weekend of September. Contestants from all 50 states and numerous foreign countries compete in eight different acoustic music contests. You'll hear traditional and progressive bluegrass, folk, country, cowboy, Celtic, blues, Cajun, and jazz on four stages. Between 30 and 40 acts perform.

Tap your feet and applaud the players' skill at the championships: International Finger-Style Guitar, International Autoharp, National Flat-Pick Guitar, National Mountain Dulcimer, National Hammered Dulcimer, National Bluegrass Banjo, National Mandolin, and the Walnut Valley Old-Time Fiddle.

The festival is not only about professional musicianship. Many attendees also play instruments. Join amateur and professional musicians during jam sessions around campsites.

Check out the juried arts and crafts fair, too.

1105 W. Ninth Ave., Winfield, KS 67156, (620) 221-3250
wvfest.com

TIP
Want more acoustic music? Come to Colby's Pickin' on the Plains festival in June at the Thomas County Fairgrounds.

(785) 460-7643, pickinontheplains.com

REVEAL THE GLORY OF THE LORD
AT THE MESSIAH FESTIVAL OF THE ARTS

On March 1, 1882, the Bethany Oratorio Society performed Handel's *Messiah* in Lindsborg. They began the longest-running annual *Messiah* performance. On Palm Sunday and Easter, the strains of G. F. Handel's masterwork echo through the Smoky Hills.

Messiah presents a three-part story: the Nativity, Christ's Passion, and the Resurrection. The oratorio includes one of the most significant choral pieces in Western music, the "Hallelujah Chorus."

On Good Friday, the society performs J. S. Bach's *St. Matthew Passion*. Bach's composition dramatizes the events leading to Christ's crucifixion using the words recorded in Matthew's gospel.

In preparation, community members and Bethany College students practice many hours in the chorus and orchestra. Many of them have performed for years, some with generations of family members. Professionals perform *The Messiah's* solo parts.

Presser Hall, 335 E. Swensson St., Lindsborg, KS 67456, (785) 227-3380
messiahfestival.org

TIP
Lindsborg celebrates the visual arts during the festival as well.
messiahfestival.org/events

TOP KANSAS ENTERTAINMENT VENUES

The New Theatre and Restaurant
Dinner theater hosts five shows annually
with five- to 13-week runs.
9229 Foster St., Overland Park, KS 66212
(913) 649-SHOW, newtheatre.com

Azura Amphitheater
Outdoor concert venue seats 18,000.
633 N. 130th St., Bonner Springs, KS 66012
(913) 825-3400, azuraamp.com

Rock Island Live
High-energy bar, restaurant, and concert venue
in downtown Wichita
101 N. Rock Island, Wichita, KS 67202
(316) 303-9800, facebook.com/RockIslandLiveMusic/

Topeka Civic Theatre and Academy
America's oldest continuously running
community dinner theatre
3028 SW Eighth Ave., Topeka, KS 66606
(785) 357-5211, topekacivictheatre.com

Boulevard Drive-In and Swap Meet
The world's first 4K drive-in cinema
1051 Merriam Ln., Kansas City, KS 66103
(913) 262-0392, boulevarddrivein.com/wordpress.com/

Kanopolis Drive-In
Sixty-foot widescreen drive-in theater
with radio-station audio
804 N. Kansas Ave., Kanopolis, KS 67454
(785) 472-4786, kanopolisdrivein.com

Midway Drive-In
Accommodates 250 cars
29591 W. 327th St., Paola, KS 66071, (913) 755-2325
facebook.com/The-Drive-In-at-Midway-
PaolaOsawatomie-101633321682827

GROW UP UNDER THE MIDWEST SKY
ON THE MELISSA ETHERIDGE TOUR

Rock star Melissa Etheridge grew up under the Midwest sky in Leavenworth. She started playing the guitar when she was eight years old, and many of her lyrics mention her hometown. In 2002, the City of Leavenworth installed a guitar-shaped sign at the city's southern entrance. It reads, "Leavenworth, KS: Hometown of Melissa Etheridge."

The fifteen stops on the Etheridge tour document Leavenworth's impact on her life and lyrics. Drive past her childhood home, see where she went to school, and visit The Tune Shop, the music store where she took lessons.

Etheridge's song "Kansas City" names Hays, Junction City, Topeka, and, of course, Kansas City. On her seventh album, she wrote an entire song, "The Prison," about the United States Penitentiary in Leavenworth. Six more places appear in her lyrics.

visitleavenworthks.com/visitors/page/melissa-etheridge-hometown-tour

---

TIP
Sharon honors its music superstar,
Martina McBride, at Martina McBride Park.

Central Ave. and Broadway St., Sharon, KS 67138

LEARN TO PLAY ANGELIC SOUNDS
AT K. C. STRINGS

Misha and Anton Krutz have created a world-class stringed instrument shop in Merriam. The store's full name is K. C. Strings Violin Shop, but don't let the name fool you. Yes, they sell violins, but they also sell violas, cellos, and basses. The Midwest's largest selection of stringed instruments, racks of cases, strings, bows, practice rooms, recital spaces, and restoration and repair services all await customers.

Misha enjoys repairing stringed instruments. Anton, a master luthier, carefully ages curly maple and spruce and then crafts the wood into superb instruments with powerful, expressive sound.

While the store sells instruments to professionals around the world, the staff welcomes student musicians. Instructors teach lessons seven days a week. Improve your musicianship at summer camps and master classes.

5842 Merriam Dr., Merriam, KS 66203, (913) 677-0400, kcstrings.com

---

TIP

At the Piano Technicians Guild's home office,
the Jack Wyatt Museum displays all things piano.

4444 Forest Ave., Kansas City, KS 66106, (913) 432-9975
ptg.org/foundation/museum/museum2

COME TOGETHER RIGHT NOW
AT THE HISTORIC STIEFEL THEATRE

Over its approximately 45-event annual season, the Stiefel Theatre for the Performing Arts attracts about 40,000 patrons to downtown Salina. Salina's central location and size has allowed the theatre to book top tours with headliners such as Jackson Browne, Chris Cornell, George Carlin, Darius Rucker, Lindsey Buckingham, Peter Frampton, Bonnie Raitt, and Emmylou Harris.

The venue opened in 1931 as the Fox-Watson Theater and was built at a cost of $400,000. The building features lavish Art Deco chandeliers, an elaborate staircase, and opulent gold leaf. In 2003, the former cinema reopened as a live performance venue.

But don't limit your experiences to bands and genres you know and favor. The Stiefel books diverse acts to expose its patrons to more than the standard fare.

Support local musicians at the Stiefel, including the Salina Symphony.

The theatre opens an hour before performances begin.

151 S. Santa Fe Ave., Salina, KS 67401, (785) 827-1998
stiefeltheatre.org

TIP
Admire the visual arts at Salina Art Center.

242 S. Santa Fe Ave., (785) 827-1431, salinaartcenter.org

● ●

DISCOVER SALINA, THE CROSSROADS OF KANSAS

Hickory Hut Barbecue
1617 W. Crawford St., Salina, KS 67401
(785) 825-1588, hickoryhut.com

Rolling Hills Zoo
625 N. Hedville Rd., Salina, KS 67401
(785) 827-9488, rollinghillszoo.org

Salina Art Cinema
150 S. Santa Fe Ave., Salina, KS 67401
(785) 827-1431, salinaartcenter.org/nowplaying

Salina Community Theatre
303 E. Iron Ave., Salina, KS 67401
(785) 827-3033, salinatheatre.com

Salina Fieldhouse
A 68,000-foot venue for multiple participatory sports
140 N. Fifth St., Salina, KS 67401
(785) 833-2260, salinafieldhouse.com

SculptureTour Salina
Twenty to 30 sculptures stand for a year.
Each year the city permanently installs the
People's Choice Award winner.
Downtown Salina, (785) 827-9301
sculpturetoursalina.net

Smoky Hill Museum
211 W. Iron Ave., Salina, KS 67401
(785) 309-5776, smokyhillmuseum.org

Smoky Hill River Festival
Oakdale Park, 730 Oakdale Dr., Salina, KS 67401
(785) 309-5770, riverfestival.com

GRAB THE BRASS RING
AT C. W. PARKER CAROUSEL MUSEUM

In 1911, Charles Wallace (C. W.) Parker moved his carousel factory to Leavenworth from Abilene. Parker's carousel business was booming. The factory workers built traveling carousels for carnivals plus extravagant machines for amusement parks.

Parker called his machines "carry-us-alls" because his company's creations entertained every age and size of passenger. Master carvers and painters created his animals and then arranged them on motorized platforms under canopies. Parker produced about 1,000 carousels. The Parkers continued their Leavenworth operations until 1955.

At the museum, visitors can ride a 1913 Parker carousel and a 1950s Paul Parker aluminum carousel. The oldest primitive carousel in the United States still runs, but is too fragile for riders. Carousel horses and parts are also displayed.

320 S. Esplanade St., Leavenworth, KS 66048, (913) 682-1331
facebook.com/ParkerCarousel

TIP
After you visit the carousels, stretch your legs in nearby Leavenworth Landing Park next to the Missouri River.

301 S. Esplanade St., (913) 651-2203
visitleavenworthks.com/visitors/page/leavenworth-landing

SPIN AROUND AT KANSAS CARNIVALS AND CAROUSELS

Carousel in the Park
SW Sixth Ave. & Gage Blvd., Topeka, KS 66606
(785) 251-6812
parks.snco.us/facilities/Facility/Details/109

The National Foundation for Carnival Heritage Center
Schedule tours with John Ploger
at Southwest Appraisal Services.
113 E. Sixth St., Kinsley, KS 67547, (620) 659-2201
edwardscounty.org/attractions.htm

The Oldest Extant C. W. Parker Carousel
Dickinson County Historical Society
412 S. Campbell St., Abilene, KS 67410, (785) 263-2681
dickinsoncountyhistoricalsociety.com/carosel

Wilmore Carousel
In the summer, drive to the carousel and honk.
If the owners are at home, they will come out
and run the carousel.
205 Main St., Wilmore, KS 67155, (620) 738-4420

SHINE IN THE LIGHT OF GLOWING SUNFLOWERS
AT KANSAS MAZE

Kansas earns the nickname "The Sunflower State" from its profuse wild sunflowers. The state also ranks fourth in commercial sunflower production, growing both oil and confectionary sunflowers. Oilseeds are smaller and black and become sunflower oil and bird seeds. Confection seeds have white stripes, and humans eat them.

Every August, the sunflowers bloom, delighting all who see hundreds of cheerful yellow flowers smiling in the fields.

Kansas Maze grows more than 16 acres of sunflowers. During the blooming season, bask in the tranquil scenery. Stroll through the fields, examining the big blooms' details and their busy pollinators.

The Sunflower Trail race course runs through the sunflowers. Shop at the Sunflower Craft Market. Kids have plenty of activities, like human foosball, a giant puzzle, and a rope maze.

13209 E. 82nd Ave., Buhler, KS 67522, (620) 543-3073
kansasmaze.com

SUNFLOWER-THEMED KANSAS ATTRACTIONS

Cedar Creek Farm
6100 N. 119th St. W, Maize, KS 67101, (316) 295-8718
cedarcreekict.com

Grinter Farms
24154 Stillwell Rd., Lawrence, KS 66044
facebook.com/GrinterFarms

Klausmeyer Farm and Pumpkin Patch
8135 S. 119th St. W, Clearwater, KS 67026
(316) 706-5391, klausmeyerdairyfarms.com

Sunflower Trails
Peterson Farm Brothers
2951 13th Ave., Lindsborg, KS 67456
petersonfarmbrothers.com/sunflower-trails

Three Sunflowers in a Vase
The World's Largest Painting on an Easel
Pioneer Park West
1998 Cherry Ave., Goodland, KS 67735
roxieontheroad.com/giant-van-gogh-painting

RELIVE A CLASSIC BOOK AND TELEVISION SHOW
AT THE *LITTLE HOUSE ON THE PRAIRIE* MUSEUM

Charles and Caroline Ingalls ride on a covered wagon as their three girls, Laura, Mary, and Carrie, run down a hill to meet them. Another episode of *Little House on the Prairie* begins. The classic television show aired on NBC for nine seasons, but it has been broadcast continually in syndication.

Cut!

Instead of the TV show's Minnesota, the Ingalls family lived here in Kansas from 1869 to 1871. Laura Ingalls Wilder wrote her classic book about the homestead. The site includes a log cabin, a schoolhouse, and a post office. The Ingalls' well is still on the property.

Instead of using the address, follow the museum's directions to the Little House (littlehouseontheprairiemuseum.com/pages/visit).

The best time to visit is Prairie Fest Days on the second Saturday in June.

2507 Rd. 3000, Independence, KS 67301, (620) 289-4238
littlehouseontheprairiemuseum.com

TIP

Independence's Neewollah (Halloween spelled backward) is the oldest festival in Kansas. The festival began in 1919. It includes the Queen Neewollah contest and the Great Pumpkin.

(877) NEE-WOLLAH
neewollah.com

RIDE THE RAILS
ON THE KANSAS BELLE DINNER TRAIN

All aboard! Embark on the Kansas Belle Dinner Train and return to the 1940s. Before widespread airline service and the interstate highway system, trains ruled long-distance passenger travel, and the dining car served fine cuisine.

When you step aboard the dinner train at the Baldwin City Depot, you'll enter a time machine. The train plays 1940s music on its 22-mile round trip through the Eastern Kansas countryside.

Saturday night runs offer a romantic three-hour tour and a five-course dinner. Bring your family for the shorter Sunday afternoon run and a three-course dinner.

For the epitome of 1940s nostalgia, add a World War II USO show to your outing. Other options include wine tastings, melodramas, and murder mysteries. During the holidays, the train presents special themed runs.

215 Ames St., Baldwin City, KS 66006, (785) 594-8505
kansasbelle.com

TIP

The Kansas Belle shares its track with the Midland Railway. The Midland carries passengers on vintage rail cars 20 miles through scenic Eastern Kansas.

1515 W. High St., (785) 594-1335, midlandrailway.org

SURVIVE A (FAKE) SHOOT-OUT
AT THE BOOT HILL MUSEUM

Dodge City came by its name, "The Queen of the Cowtowns," honestly. Between 1875 and 1885, a million cattle came through Dodge City.

Like all cowtowns, Dodge City was wild. In one year, 1875, 25 people died from gunshot wounds—and Dodge City had outlawed firearms. The city attracted famous gunmen: Wyatt Earp, the Masterson brothers, Bill Tilghman, Clay Allison, Luke Short, Dave Mather, and "Doc" Holliday all lived in Dodge.

Experience Dodge City's wild side in a G-rated version at the Boot Hill Museum. Take an old-time portrait at Old West Photo. During the summer, gunfighters slug and shoot each other. Watch dancing girls perform in the Long Branch Variety Show. Get some relief from summer's heat in the Beatty and Kelley Ice Cream Parlor.

500 W. Wyatt Earp Blvd., Dodge City, KS 67801, (620) 227-8188
boothill.org

TIP
Boot Hill Museum offers sarsaparilla.
For adult beverages, head to Dodge City Brewing.
701 Third Ave., (620) 371-3999, dodgecitybrewing.com

CHOOSE YOUR WOODEN THRONE
ON THE ELK FALLS OUTHOUSE TOUR

Elk Falls is the Outhouse Capital of the World. It got the title when a committee was seeking a community distinction. During the meeting, someone joked about the community's outhouses. The committee decided to hold an Elk Falls Outhouse Tour during their annual open house.

The outhouses became a permanent part of the event held the Friday and Saturday before Thanksgiving.

Each year, participants construct, remodel, and decorate their outhouses according to a theme. The top three receive cash prizes. The winner earns the Outhouse Throne Award, a custom-made pottery chamber pot.

Buy a festival button, pick up a ballot and map at the downtown Outhouse Headquarters, and vote for your favorite outhouses.

Other festival events include the Harvest Craft Fair, Quilt Show, and the Vintage Camper Gathering.

712 Seventh St., Elk Falls, KS 67345, (620) 642-2112, elkfallsouthousetour.com

---

TIP
Steve and Jane Fry of Elk Falls Pottery
dig their own clay and handcraft all of their work.

1954 Hwy. 160, (620) 329-4425, elkfallspottery.com

JOIN THE PARTY
AT THE CHRISTMAS CITY OF THE HIGH PLAINS

Before each Thanksgiving, WaKeeney prepares to become the Christmas City of the High Plains. The city hangs lights and garlands and stands its gigantic, 35-foot Christmas tree in the center of downtown WaKeeney.

On the magical Saturday after Thanksgiving, the festivities begin.

During the day, shop at the Christmas Bazaar, tour the holiday display at the Trego County Historical Museum, and walk the WaKeeney Main Street Nature Trail.

Visit the countryside on your way to Shiloh Vineyard south of Voda. But don't take too long: the lighting ceremony starts at 6 p.m.

Follow the crowds to the lighting ceremony. Then listen for the jingle bells as Santa arrives to inspect the lights and greet his fans. Afterward, savor a steak at the Western Kansas Saloon & Grill, 121 N. Main, (785) 743-2050.

408 Russell Ave., WaKeeney, KS 67762, (785) 743-8325, wakeeney.org

---

TIP

Every December, Wreaths Across America decorates graves at veteran's cemeteries, including WaKeeney's Kansas Veterans Cemetery.

403 S. 13th St., (785) 743-5685
kcva.ks.gov/veteran-cemeteries/wakeeney

Mt. Sunflower north of Weskan,
Kansas's highest point

SPORTS AND RECREATION

EXPERIENCE THE ORIGINAL RULES OF BASKETBALL
AT THE DEBRUCE CENTER

James Naismith, basketball's inventor, started coaching basketball at the University of Kansas in 1898. In 2010, David Booth bought Naismith's original "Rules of Basketball" for $4.3 million and donated them to his alma mater. The rules' new home, The DeBruce Center, opened in 2016.

Naismith's student Forrest "Phog" Allen coached the Jayhawks for 40 years after Naismith retired. Allen, the father of basketball coaching, created the NCAA basketball tournament.

The Rules Gallery explains KU's connection to basketball. While at the center, learn about basketball equipment's evolution, meet those enshrined in the Naismith Hall of Fame, and watch videos about the sport's history.

Next door is the Booth Family Hall of Athletics, where fans can experience KU's history and tradition. Admire KU basketball's championship trophy case and various interactive exhibits.

1647 Naismith Dr., Lawrence, KS 66045, (785) 864-9750
debrucecenter.ku.edu

TIP

Visit Naismith's grave in Memorial Park Cemetery, 1517 E. 15th Street, Lawrence. You'll find his picture engraved on his stone with a Jayhawk logo medallion below.

CHANT
"ROCK CHALK JAYHAWK"
AT KU GAMES

When the University of Kansas Jayhawks are on the floor, prepare to hear the mesmerizing, spine-chilling chant, "Rock Chalk Jayhawk, KU!" repeatedly.

In 1886, chemistry professor E. H. S. Bailey experimented with a chant for his science club, patterning the cadence after a train rolling down the tracks. His version was "Ray, Rah, Jay Hawk, KU." An English professor suggested that "Ray, Rah" change to "Rock Chalk." "Rock Chalk" rhymes with "Jayhawk" and pays homage to the chalk rock that makes up the campus on Lawrence's Mount Oread. In 1887, the edited chant became official. Initially, chanters repeat a drawn-out cadence twice and then say it three times in a staccato style.

Fans have rained down the chant for 14 national titles, including five in men's basketball.

Allen Fieldhouse, 1651 Naismith Dr., Lawrence, KS 66045, (785) 864-3417
kuathletics.com/traditions

TIP

The Jayhawk, KU's mascot, came from a Civil War regiment, the Independent Mounted Jayhawkers. The bird's appearance took its current form in 1946.

"WABASH" DURING "THE WABASH CANNONBALL"
AT K-STATE GAMES

On December 13, 1968, arsonists burned down Kansas State University's Department of Music. The fire torched nearly all of the Pride of Wildcat Land's band music. "The Wabash Cannonball" was the band's sole surviving sheet music—because the director, Phil Hewett, had taken home a copy. The band had to perform three days later at a men's basketball game. Hewett copied the song and borrowed instruments from Manhattan High School. The band played the selection over and over that night and birthed a tradition.

Woodwinds have no part in the tune's first half, so they lead the fans in a dance. To do the Wabash, turn to the left and right like your Wildcat neighbors. Then bob forward and backward, opposite of your neighbors.

K-State athletics complex, 1800 College Ave., Manhattan, KS 66502,
(785) 532-6910, kstatesports.com

TIP

Celebrate Wildcat football game day with
Visit Manhattan's Game Day Guide.

manhattancvb.org/events/kansas-state-gameday

SHOCK YOUR OPPONENTS
WITH WICHITA STATE'S WUSHOCK

In 2017, fans voted Wichita State's seven-foot tall mascot WuShock as the nation's best on CollegeCourtReport.com. No other university uses the Shocker team name.

The Shockers earned their name from many players who shocked (harvested) wheat in the summers. In 1904, R. J. Kirk, the football manager, needed to advertise a game. He invented the name Wheatshockers. Later the university shortened the mascot's name to Shockers.

In 1948, Wilbur Elsea won a contest for a Wichita athletics logo. He said, "The school needed a mascot who gave a tough impression, with a serious, no-nonsense scowl." Jack Kersting devised the mascot's name, WuShock. Wu stands for Wichita University. In 1954, cheerleader David Johnson created WuShock's first costume.

An eight-foot WuShock sculpture stands in front of the Steve Clark YMCA.

2060 N. Mid-Campus Dr., Wichita, KS 67208, (316) 776-8370
wichita.edu/about/wushock.php

TIP
Buy tickets for Shocker athletics at goshockers.com/sports/tickets.

EMBRACE THE BEAUTIFUL GAME
WITH SPORTING KANSAS CITY

Soccer, popular the world over, is nicknamed "The Beautiful Game." Soccer features unpredictable action and visually pleasing motions, and it creates communities. Championships are beautiful, too. The Kansas City soccer club has stood atop Major League Soccer twice, in 2000 and 2013.

For the best experience, join the Cauldron. Tailgate in Lot F. The Cauldron seating is in sections M1–M9, but participate wherever you are. After the national anthem, fans often do a prearranged choreographed display (called a tifo). If you don't know what to do, do what the person next to you does.

Stand up the entire match, join the chants, sing the songs, and wave the flags when Sporting KC scores. When the cannons shoot confetti, it's time to celebrate with hugs, high fives, yelling, dancing, and chest-bumping.

Children's Mercy Park, One Sporting Way, Kansas City, KS 66111
(888) 4KC-GOAL, sportingkc.com

TIP
Wear the proper apparel to the match.
Shop at mlsstore.com/sporting-kansas-city.

PAY HOMAGE
TO GOLF'S GREAT HOLES
AT FIREKEEPER GOLF COURSE

PGA Tour pro Notah Begay III collaborated with golf architect Jeffrey D. Bauer to design Firekeeper Golf Course. Begay is the only full-blooded Native American to play on the PGA Tour, and Firekeeper is on the Prairie Band of Potawatomi Nation Reservation. The design team worked with the rolling hills instead of fighting the landscape.

The fourth hole gives nods to the Royal St. Georges's fourth hole and the 11th hole at the Los Angeles Country Club. The ninth hole imitates Augusta National's 18th hole.

The windsocks at the holes display the wind direction, important where the wind rarely ceases. Note the course's subtle elevation changes.

Bauer also designed Colbert Hills Golf Course in Manhattan and Sand Creek Station Golf Course in Newton.

12524 150th Rd., Mayetta, KS 66509, (785) 966-2100
firekeepergolf.com

TIP

Firekeeper is across the road from the Prairie Band Casino & Resort.

12305 150th Rd., (785) 966-7777, prairieband.com

SHRED THE DUNES
AT SYRACUSE SAND DUNES PARK

Dunes in Kansas? Oh, yes! Bash those dunes at Syracuse Sand Dunes Park, Kansas's largest dunes park. The Arkansas River and Kansas wind have laid down the sand over millennia. Some of the dunes are 50 feet high. They're like riding a roller coaster.

Thirteen hundred acres of dunes, hills, bowls, and flat areas await you on the park's expansive sand trails. Get ready to roll in the park's large staging area.

Catch your dinner in Sam's Pond, a 40-acre fishing hole. Catfish, carp, largemouth bass, bluegill, crappie, and perch swim in the pond. From October to April, catch rainbow trout. Anglers must have a Kansas fishing license.

Stay in the park at any of 14 RV campsites around the pond or bring tents to use dry camping spaces.

55 W. River Rd., Syracuse, KS 67878, (620) 384-2480
syracusesanddunespark.com

TIP
On the other side of the state, go off-road in the Ozark Plateau at Kansas Rocks Recreation Park.
2051 130th Rd., Mapleton, KS 66754, (620) 829-5328
ksrockspark.com

SATISFY YOUR NEED FOR SPEED
AT THE KANSAS SPEEDWAY

Speed demons need to experience the Kansas Speedway. Watch the professionals race during two NASCAR Cup Series races, truck races, and more. The speedway packs in 72,000 fans around the 1.5-mile tri-oval course. The infield holds a six-turn 2.37-mile road course.

But committed speed demons will want to drive, not watch. The solution: drive a NASCAR race car on the speedway with the NASCAR Racing Experience. After meeting with a crew chief, get behind the wheel without a lead car or an instructor. A spotter will instruct you via the in-car radio. The sessions last eight minutes, with pit stops in between. As you figure out how to fly low, zoom around the slower cars.

Do you feel the rush? Oh, yeah!

400 Speedway Blvd., Kansas City, KS 66111, (704) 886-2400
nascarracingexperience.com/kansas-speedway

TIP
Celebrate Race Day in style with extra fan experiences.
kansasspeedway.com/Buy-Tickets/Fan-Experiences.aspx

SPEED THRILLS AT KANSAS MOTOR SPORTS VENUES

Dodge City Raceway Park
11322 110th Rd., Dodge City, KS 67801
(620) 225-3277, dodgecityraceway.com

Heartland Motor Sports Park
7530 SW Topeka Blvd., Topeka, KS 66619
(785) 861-7899, heartlandmotorsports.us

Kansas Auto Racing Museum
1205 Manor Dr., Chapman, KS 67431
(785) 922-6642, kansasautoracingmuseum.org

Kansas International Dragway
7800 W. 61st St. N, Maize, KS 67101
(316) 833-4556, kansasdragway.com

Lakeside Speedway
5615 Wolcott Dr., Kansas City, KS 66109
(913) 299-9206, lakesidespeedway.net

SCRA Dragstrip
Home of the first NHRA Nationals in 1955
455 W. Barton County Rd., Great Bend, KS 67530
(620) 792-5079, srcadragstrip.com

GET YOUR KICKS
ON KANSAS ROUTE 66

The fabled Mother Road, Route 66, crosses the southeastern corner of Kansas. The 13.2-mile stretch is the shortest section in any state, but don't miss it. There's plenty to experience.

The hit movie *Cars* renewed interest in the iconic road. *Cars* director John Lasseter found Tow Tater at Cars on the Route in Galena, inspiring the warm-hearted character Tow Mater. The sheriff welcomes visitors at Galena's eastern entrance. Take pictures in cutouts of Dorothy and Toto, Fillmore, and more.

The Eisler Bros. Old Riverton Store features a comprehensive Route 66 souvenir selection. Drive an original Route 66 section between Riverton and Baxter Springs.

Look for the Route 66 Visitor Center's Phillips 66 pole sign and gas pumps in Baxter Springs. Visit the Decades of Wheels Museum and Spin Out Arcade.

Route 66 Association of Kansas, 7109 Hwy. 66, Riverton, KS 66770
(620) 848-3330, eislerbros.com

TIP
Relish the chicken-fried steak at Van's Steakhouse.
2447 Military Ave., Baxter Springs, KS 66713, (620) 856-5506
facebook.com/vansbaxter

COLLECT A DOZEN KANSAS BYWAYS

travelks.com/ksbyways

**Flint Hills National
Scenic Byway**
47 miles, (620) 273-8469

**Frontier Military
Historic Byway**
168 miles
(913) 758-2948

**Glacial Hills
Scenic Byway**
63 miles, (800) 234-1854

**Gypsum Hills
Scenic Byway**
42 miles, (620) 886-9815

**Land and Sky
Scenic Byway**
88 miles, (785) 332-3508

**Native Stone
Scenic Byway**
75 miles, (785) 220-4634

Post Rock Scenic Byway
18 miles, (785) 525-6288

**Prairie Trail
Scenic Byway**
80 miles, (620) 242-7133

**Historic Route 66
Byway**
13 miles, (620) 674-8449

**Smoky Valley
Scenic Byway**
60 miles, (785) 743-8325

**Western Vistas
Historic Byway**
102 miles
(620) 874-0174

**Wetlands and Wildlife
National Scenic Byway**
77 miles, (620) 792-2750

PADDLE THE REAL KANSAS
ON THE KANSAS RIVER TRAIL

Driving Interstate 70 deceives travelers into believing that Kansas is treeless and flat. Paddling the Kansas River Trail will unwind the stereotype. Watch as the geology and climate change along the river.

Glaciers carved out the river and moved rocks far from their origins. Ice Age fossils appear on the river's sandbars, especially after high-water events.

Woodlands surround the lower river from Lawrence to Kansas City. The trees increase as the river leaves the Flint Hills around its beginning at Junction City.

Wade, kayak, and canoe in the river, but do not swim or water ski. Wash your hands frequently, especially before eating. World-class catfish swim in the river. Flathead catfish are the most common, but channel cats and blue ones are there, too. Do not eat fish caught between Lawrence and Eudora.

PO Box 1612, Lawrence, KS 66044, (785) 312-7200
kansasriver.org

TIP

View a map and learn tips for novices and advanced paddlers.
kansasriver.org/river-access-map

EXTEND YOUR KANSAS RIVER ADVENTURE

The Kansas River is also known as the Kaw River.

Kaw Point Park

Meriwether Lewis and William Clark's Corps of Discovery camped at the Kaw's conjunction with the Missouri River on June 26, 1804.
1 River City Dr., Kansas City, KS 66115
(913) 677-2088, nps.gov/articles/kaw-point-park.htm

Kaw River State Park

300 SW Wanamaker Rd., Topeka, KS 66615
(785) 273-6740
ksoutdoors.com/State-Parks/Locations/Kaw-River

Louis Vieux Cemetery and Oregon Trail Nature Park

20560 Oregon Trail Rd., Wamego, KS 66547
visitwamego.com/see-and-do/oregon-trail

Perry Lake National Recreation Trail

Rugged 30-mile trail on Perry Lake's eastern side
10419 Perry Park Dr., Perry, KS 66073
(785) 597-5144
recreation.gov/camping/gateways/271

TEST YOUR MOUNTAIN-BIKING SKILLS
ON THE SWITCHGRASS BIKE TRAIL

Colorado and Utah don't have a red-rock trails monopoly. The Switchgrass Bike Trail is the only epic-rated trail in Kansas, with nearly 25 miles of red rocks, sand, ledges, and drops. However, most of the technical sections are short.

The single-track trail design features three stacked loops with a dozen forks. You must ride the loops in succession. The Golden Belt Loop is first, followed by the Marina Loop and the Hell Creek Loop. To ride the entire trail, always take the left fork. To shorten the ride, head right at any fork.

Dakota sandstone fills the Golden Belt's first four miles. Brokebike Mountain highlights the Marina Loop. Pass under the Hell Creek Bridge to start the Hell Creek Loop and back around to the trailhead.

Wilson State Park, 3 State Park Rd., Sylvan Grove, KS 67481
(785) 658-2465, facebook.com/SwitchgrassTrail

TIP
Use the Dorrance (199) or Wilson (206) exit from I-70 and find the Hell Creek Area at Wilson State Park. Check trail conditions on the Facebook page.

GRIND SOME GRAVEL
DURING THE GARMIN UNBOUND GRAVEL 200

Can you endure 200 miles of rugged, lonely Flint Hills gravel road during the World's Premier Gravel Event—for up to 19 grueling hours? Can you overcome the weather, the terrain, your body—and your mind? Then join the 4,000 riders who pour through Emporia's streets into the Flint Hills on the first weekend after Memorial Day. Hardcore cyclists endure a 350-mile race.

Not so hardcore? Then choose from the 25-, 50-, or 100-mile races. Students have a separate race.

Would you rather stand by the road and cheer? Then join thousands more who join Emporia's festivities. Find everything you need for gravel grinding and celebrating at the All Things Gravel Expo. The fun starts in the afternoon and goes far into the night.

unboundgravel.com

TIP

Biking Across Kansas sponsors an eight-day cycling tour across the state each June. The route differs each year and has visited nearly every corner of the state.

PO Box 192, Olathe, KS 66051, (913) 735-3035, bak.org

ENTER
A BIRDER'S PARADISE
AT CHEYENNE BOTTOMS

"Fuh-rawhrr! Fuh-rawhrr! Fuh-rawhrr!" Thousands of sandhill cranes voice their spring mating song as they dance at Cheyenne Bottoms near Great Bend. The cranes and millions of other migratory birds stop at the bottoms each year, flying from as far away as Tierra del Fuego. The area attracts 45 percent of North American shorebirds during spring migration.

As the world's largest inland marsh, Cheyenne Bottoms looks like a giant's thumbprint on the earth: a thumbprint teeming with birds. The Nature Conservancy and Kansas Department of Wildlife and Parks manage nearly 28,000 acres of habitat.

Start your tour at the Kansas Wetlands Education Center and examine the exhibits. Join a guided tour or pick up a self-guided tour brochure. Bring your spotting scopes.

592 NE Hwy. 156, Great Bend, KS 67530, (620) 566-1456
wetlandscenter.fhsu.edu

TIP

The center hosts the Wings and Wetlands Birding Festival
in the spring of odd-numbered years.

DESTINATIONS FOR THE BIRDS

Bird City, Kansas is not named for its avian population, but it is the only incorporated "Bird City" in the nation. Visit these five preserves full of amazing avians.

Baker Wetlands & Discovery Center
1365 N. 1250 Rd., Lawrence, KS 66046
(785) 594-4700
bakeru.edu/history-traditions/the-wetlands

Jamestown Wildlife Area
209 Marsh Trail, Jamestown, KS 66948
(785) 439-6243
ksoutdoors.com/KDWPT-Info/Locations/Wildlife-
Areas/Northwest/Jamestown

Kirwin National Wildlife Refuge
702 E. Xavier Rd., Kirwin, KS 67644, (785) 543-6673
fws.gov/refuge/kirwin

Marais des Cygnes National Wildlife Refuge
16382 Hwy. 69, Pleasanton, KS 66075
(913) 352-8956, fws.gov/refuge/marais_des_cygnes

Quivira National Wildlife Refuge
1434 NE 80th St., Stafford, KS 67578
(620) 486-2393, fws.gov/refuge/quivira

REEL IN THE BIG ONE
AT MILFORD RESERVOIR

Numerous fishing tournaments come to Milford Reservoir. A 6.88-pound, state-record smallmouth bass came from Milford. If you're an angler, go where the championship fish swim. Expect to catch something every time you make the trip. With 5,700 acres of lake and over 160 shoreline miles, you'll find a fishing hole. Pursue bass, catfish, walleye, crappie, sunfish, sauger, white bass, and wipers.

All of the fishing infrastructure is present. Marina: check. Boat ramp: check. Bait and tackle: check.

See where your fish hatch at the Milford Nature Center and Fish Hatchery. Learn how to bring nature home to your backyard at the nature center.

Why are you waiting? Grab your rod and reel, buy a fishing license, and go to Milford.

Find more fishing holes at ksoutdoors.com/Fishing/Where-to-Fish-in-Kansas.

8811 State Park Rd., Milford, KS 66514, (785) 238-3014
junctioncity.org/58/Milford-Lake

TIP

Stay at Acorns Resort & RV Park and
get all you need for a successful Milford adventure.

3710 Farnum Creek Rd., (785) 463-4000, acornsresortkansas.com

---

MARVEL AT KANSAS CANYONS
IN THE ARIKAREE BREAKS

Tucked into the northwest corner of Kansas, the Arikaree Breaks defy the (false) notion that Kansas is flat. During the Ice Age, glaciers ground the soil into fine particles called loess (pronounced "LUSS"). In Cheyenne County, the wind-carved sharp canyons twist and turn across the land. The canyons expose ash-grey rocks from the water-bearing Ogallala Formation.

In the spring, yucca blooms and numerous sagebrush varieties accent the dramatic landforms. On the Breaks's west side, a herd of buffalo grazes.

At first, the Arikaree Breaks scenic drive looks like any ordinary country drive. But wait. Soon, the landscape changes dramatically.

Check road conditions and pick up a map. Before you leave, fill up your gas tank and fortify your stomach at Fresh Seven Coffee, 312 W. Washington Street, (785) 772-0823, freshsevencoffee.com.

Cheyenne County Development Corporation
107 W. Washington St., St. Francis, KS 67756, (785) 332-3508
ccdcks.com/index.php?page=explore

TIP
Also visit the St. Francis Motorcycle Museum.

110 E. Washington St., (785) 332-2400
stfrancismotorcyclemuseum.org

ROCK YOUR WORLD
AT LITTLE JERUSALEM BADLANDS STATE PARK

Primordial seas have drowned Kansas, glaciers have scoured her, winds have scrubbed her, and floods have drenched her. The geological shocks have left fascinating imprints on the land. Little Jerusalem Badlands State Park is one of the state's most scenic wonders.

The Western Interior Sea laid down Niobrara Chalk. Tectonics uplifted the chalk, and wind eroded it into dramatic shapes. Settlers named the formations "Little Jerusalem."

Two trails wind through the formations. Please stay on them and do not touch the fragile rocks. The quarter-mile Overlook Trail ends at a park bench. The 1.2-mile Life on the Rocks Trail crosses a creek on its way to two overlooks and the most dramatic view. As the sun's angle changes during the day, the rocks' appearance changes, too.

Gold Rd. and Rd. 400, Oakley, KS 67748, (620) 872-2061
ksoutdoors.com/State-Parks/Locations/Little-Jerusalem-Badlands

---

TIP

The park is Kansas's most significant exposed Niobrara Chalk formation. More formations pepper the landscape along the Smoky Hill River from Trego County to Wallace County.

ROCK KANSAS WITH THESE FORMATIONS

Do not climb the rocks. Cell service may be spotty or non-existent. Check road conditions before you go.

Castle Rock
Hike the adjoining Castle Rock Badlands.
Roads K and 80, Quinter, KS 67752, (785) 743-8325
naturalkansas.org/castle.htm

Monument Rocks
Kansas's first National Natural Landmark
Rd. 16, Oakley, KS 67748, (785) 671-1000
facebook.com/Monument-Rocks-Chalk-Pyramids-Kansas-368367609970440

Mushroom Rocks State Park
Three miles west of Hwy. 141 on Ave. K, Carneiro, KS 67425
(785) 546-2565
ksoutdoors.com/State-Parks/Locations/Mushroom-Rock

Rock City
World's largest rock concretions
1051 Ivy Rd., Minneapolis, KS 67467, (785) 392-2092
geokansas.ku.edu/rock-city

Rocktown Trail
Three-mile loop trail passing 15- to 30-foot tall rock formations at Wilson State Park
Interstate 70 Wilson Exit 206, (785) 658-2551
getoutdoorskansas.org/trails/wilson-lake-rocktown-trail

Amelia Earhart Birthplace Museum, Atchison

Dwight Eisenhower at the Eisenhower Museum, Library and Boyhood Home, Abilene

Keyhole at Monument Rocks National
Natural Landmark south of Oakley

The Rainbow Bridge over
Brush Creek west of Riverton

Little Rock Central High School exhibit at the Lowell Milken Center for Unsung Heroes, Fort Scott

Kansas State Capitol, Topeka

Mini-Grand Canyon in the Arikaree Breaks

Detail of "El Baile de la Vida (The Dance of Life),"
Avenue of Murals, Minnesota Ave., Kansas City

The Keeper of the Plains, Wichita

Ripening wheat on Land and Sky Scenic
Byway south of Goodland

K. C. Strings, Merriam

Wildflowers at Konza Prairie

Wheat field south of Quinter

Z-Bar Ranch at Tallgrass Prairie
National Preserve north of Strong City

UNEARTH GIANT FOSSILS
AT THE STERNBERG MUSEUM

A terrifying *Tyrannosaurus rex* stands with arms outstretched, talons extended, growling at the humans that walk by. No, this is not Jurassic Park. It's the Sternberg Museum of Natural History. The museum's diorama depicts the Late Cretaceous Epoch. If you dare, dive into the Western Interior Sea, where the monsters *Xiphactinus* and *Tylosaurus* troll for prey.

George F. Sternberg gave the museum its name. In 1927, Fort Hays State University hired him as a paleontologist and museum curator. He excavated the 14-foot *Xiphactinus audax* skeleton with a six-foot fish inside. The Fish-within-a-Fish hangs in the museum's fossil gallery.

Other exhibits include Ice Age fossils and Bringing Fossils to Life, comparing fossils and their present-day descendants. Not all the displays are dead. Live rattlesnakes inhabit the "Rattlerssss" exhibit.

3000 Sternberg Dr., Hays, KS 67601, (877) 332-1165
sternberg.fhsu.edu

TIP
Join a fossil-hunting excursion at the Keystone Gallery.

401 Hwy. 83, Scott City, KS 67871, (620) 872-2762
keystonegallery.com

ASCEND KANSAS'S HIGHEST POINT
AT MOUNT SUNFLOWER

You won't need climbing gear to summit 4,039-foot Mount Sunflower, because the road leads straight to the summit. The table begs you to pack a picnic. Arrive shortly before sunset and stay for the stars. The peaceful scene may include some of Ed and Cindy Harold's cattle, so beware of manure.

While you're waiting for sunset, visit the Fort Wallace Museum, 2655 Highway 40, Wallace, KS 67761, (785) 891-3564, ftwallace.com.

The fort's soldiers saw plenty of action, earning the title "The Fightingest Fort in the West." Fossil-hunting post surgeon Theophilus Turner discovered a plesiosaur east of the fort, and the toothy swimmer's replica hangs in the museum. The Fort Wallace Cemetery, two miles southeast of the museum, is the fort's sole remnant.

Shop and eat in Wallace and Sharon Springs.

N. Third Rd. and Washboard Rd., Weskan, KS 67762
facebook.com/Mount-Sunflower-225447390834

TIP
Before you visit Mount Sunflower, check the mountain's Facebook page for road conditions and download a map.

roxieontheroad.com/wp-content/uploads/2020/05/Mt-Sunflower.pdf

---

ESCAPE MODERNITY
AT KONZA PRAIRIE
BIOLOGICAL STATION

Interstate 70 traffic whizzes by south of Konza Prairie Biological Station, and Manhattan is but 10 miles away. Both are visible from the summits of Konza Prairie's many heights. But engine sounds don't penetrate there. Natural sounds surround hikers instead.

Watch the herons stalk the creeks, and see the hawks glide on the thermals above.

Three trails thread through the Konza: the 2.6-mile Nature Trail, the 4.6-mile Kings Creek Loop, and the 6.2-mile Godwin Hill Loop.

Allow 2 hours for the Nature Trail, 3.5 for Kings Creek, and 4.5 for Godwin Hill. The trails close at dark; plan accordingly. Bring water and snacks. Bathrooms and trash cans are available only at the trailhead and the Hokanson Homestead.

100 Konza Prairie Ln., Manhattan, KS 66502, (785) 587-0381
naturalkansas.org/konza.htm

TIP
Learn what makes the Flint Hills extraordinary
at the Flint Hills Discovery Center.

315 S. Third St., (785) 587-2726, flinthillsdiscovery.org

HEARKEN TO THE SINGING GRASS
AT THE TALLGRASS PRAIRIE NATIONAL PRESERVE

In the fall, the native tallgrass can reach six feet tall along the riverbanks and five feet tall on the hills. The grass swirls and dances with its partner, the wind. The wind and grass whisper and breathe deeply before they start singing a duet.

Tallgrass prairie used to sing on 170 million North American acres, but only four percent of it remains intact. The 11,000-acre Tallgrass Prairie Preserve is one of the few venues where the tallgrass still sings.

Explore the historic ranch, the visitor center with native grasses planted on its roof, join a bus tour to see bison, and hike the trails.

We enjoy hiking the Legacy Trail from the visitor center to the Z Bar Ranch and the Lower Fox Creek School.

2480B Hwy. 177, Strong City, KS 66869, (620) 273-8494
nps.gov/tapr

TIP
Hikers may cross the pastures where
the bison roam, but read the safety tips first.

nps.gov/tapr/planyourvisit/safety.htm

ROAM WHERE THE BUFFALO CALL HOME
AT MAXWELL WILDLIFE REFUGE

With a little imagination, visitors can return to the virgin prairie at Maxwell Wildlife Refuge. American bison and elk roam among many species of grasses. Watching the grasses wave in the wind as insects flitter above is magical enough, but adding in the big beasts makes the experience extraordinary. The grasses here make up a Kansas grass hall of fame: big bluestem, little bluestem, Indiangrass, switchgrass, and side oats grama. In the spring, native sand plum bushes bloom. Book a tram tour to get close to the bison.

The McPherson State Fishing Lake a mile east of the refuge is a prime wildflower viewing spot in the spring. Coneflowers, purple prairie clover, yucca, and yellow star grass adorn the landscape. Milkweed attracts butterflies.

2565 Pueblo Rd., Canton, KS 67428, (620) 654-7230
maxwellwildliferefuge.com

TIP
Follow agriculture's mechanization at
the Mennonite Heritage and Agricultural Museum a few miles away.

200 N. Poplar St., Goessel, KS 67053, (620) 367-8200
goesselmuseum.com

SAVING THE KANSAS STATE MAMMAL FROM EXTINCTION

Until 1867, vast bison (or buffalo) herds roamed the continent. By 1902, hunting and habitat destruction had left only 700 wild bison. Private individuals began breeding bison. Combined with the small remaining wild herds, the species evaded extinction.

Beaver Creek Buffalo
Order delicious buffalo meat.
PO Box 102, Goodland, KS 67735, (785) 899-9274
beavercreekbuffalo.com

Buffalo Bill Cultural Center
William F. "Buffalo Bill" Cody won his nickname in a bison-shooting contest nearby.
3083 Hwy. 83, Oakley, KS 67748, (785) 671-1000
buffalobilloakley.org

The Bison's Savior, Charles J. "Buffalo" Jones
Finney County Historical Museum
403 S. Fourth St., Garden City, KS 67846
(620) 272-3664, finneycounty.org/171/Exhibits

Hays Bison Herd at Frontier Park West
Hwy. 183 Alt. and Golf Course Rd., Hays, KS 67601
(785) 628-7375, visithays.com/193/Bison-Herd

Sandsage Bison Range and Wildlife Area
The oldest publicly-owned herd in Kansas
785 S. Hwy. 83, Garden City, KS 67846
(620) 276-9400, fosbrgc.wixsite.com/fosbr

Smoky Valley Ranch
1114 Rd. 370, Oakley, KS 67748, (785) 233-4400
nature.org/en-us/get-involved/how-to-help/places-we-protect/smoky-valley-ranch/

Big Brutus, West Mineral

CULTURE AND HISTORY

FOLLOW THE YELLOW BRICK ROAD
TO THE EMERALD CITY OF OZ

The entire history of Oz unfolds at the Oz Museum in Wamego. MGM's iconic 1939 film *The Wizard of Oz* was not the first movie to dramatize L. Frank Baum's books. Oz came to movieland during the silent era. The museum holds memorabilia of all the Oz adaptations, from Baum's first editions to *Wicked*.

Gaze in awe at the 50th anniversary Ruby Slippers, covered with 3,500 Swarovski crystals.

To enter the museum, walk the Yellow Brick Road. Just like in the 1939 movie, the gift shop entrance is sepia-toned. Deck your home with every sort of Oz gear.

The official Road to Oz begins at Interstate 70's Exit 328 onto Highway 99. From the exit, drive north to Wamego.

511 Lincoln Ave., Wamego, KS 66547, (785) 458-8686
ozmuseum.com

TIP

Before he founded an automotive giant, Walter P. Chrysler lived in Wamego and Ellis. See Chrysler-themed exhibits at the Wamego Historical Society & Museum, 406 E. Fourth Street, Wamego, KS 66547, wamegohistoricalmuseum.org/village.html, and his boyhood home at 102 W. 10th Street, Ellis, KS 67637, facebook.com/Walter-P-Chrysler-Boyhood-Home-Museum-250622715086532.

SEE THE WIZARD, THE WONDERFUL WIZARD OF OZ

Dorothy's House & Land of Oz
567 E. Cedar St., Liberal, KS 67901, (620) 624-7624
dorothyshouse.com/dorothy-s-house.html

Oz Winery
417 Lincoln Ave., Wamego, KS 66547
(785) 456-7417, ozwinerykansas.com

Oztoberfest and Totos Around Town
Downtown Wamego, (785) 456-7849
visitwamego.com/events
visitwamego.com/totos-around-town

Toto's TacOZ
515 Lincoln Ave., Wamego, KS 66547
(785) 456-8090, totostacoz.com

**The World's Longest Yellow Brick Road and
The Yellow Brick Road Festival**
Downtown Sedan, KS 67361, (620) 725-4033
travelks.com/listing/yellow-brick-road/11782

LIKE IKE
AT THE EISENHOWER
PRESIDENTIAL LIBRARY

Decorated general and US president Dwight Eisenhower once said, "The proudest thing I can claim is that I am from Abilene."

Dwight "Ike" Eisenhower was one of the 20th century's most famous people. He commanded the Allied Expeditionary Force in Europe in World War II, then served two terms as President.

Eisenhower's Presidential campaign advertising used the slogan "I Like Ike." And the American people did like Ike, with his trademark wide, friendly grin. Among other achievements, Eisenhower proposed the Interstate Highway System. Appropriately, Abilene is on Interstate 70. He also championed peace and civil rights.

At the Eisenhower Library, follow Ike's life from his boyhood days until his family laid him to rest. The Eisenhowers lived in the house from 1898 until his mother Ida died. At the museum, hear Ike and his wife Mamie's stories in their own words.

200 SE Fourth St., Abilene, KS 67410, (785) 263-6700
eisenhowerlibrary.gov

TIP

Eisenhower defeated Democrat Adlai Stevenson twice for President. All those who ran for President and lost, including Stevenson and Kansans Alf Landon and Robert Dole, are featured in the "They Also Ran" gallery in Norton's First State Bank.

105 W. Main St., Norton, KS 67654
(785) 877-3341, theyalsoran.com

FLY ABOVE CONVENTION
WITH AMELIA EARHART

Amelia Earhart was born to fly—and to defy convention. She built a roller coaster on top of her grandparents' home in Atchison. When the coaster tipped over, Earhart was undaunted. "It felt just like flying," she said. Proper ladies didn't build roller coasters—or fly airplanes.

After Earhart learned to fly, she assaulted aviation's record books. In 1932, she flew solo across the Atlantic in record time. She was the first woman to fly nonstop from coast to coast and the first solo pilot to fly from Honolulu to Oakland, California.

On June 1, 1937, she took off on an around-the-world flight with her navigator Fred Noonan. On July 2, the pair disappeared before they could land on Howland Island in the Pacific. The mystery tantalizes searchers even now.

223 N. Terrace St., Atchison, KS 66002, (913) 367-4217
ameliaearhartmuseum.org

TIP

Atchison honors its most famous citizen with two museums, a forest, an earthwork, and a festival. visitatchison.com

---

BLAST OFF TO THE FINAL FRONTIER
AT THE COSMOSPHERE

Legendary spacecraft like Apollo 13 pack the exhibition galleries of the Cosmosphere in Hutchinson. From a planetarium set up at the Kansas State Fair, the museum has grown to include the world's most extensive collection of American and Russian space artifacts.

Journey through space flight's beginnings with one-of-a-kind artifacts. Germany's Vengeance weapons were the first human-made objects to reach space. Sputnik was the first artificial satellite. Its launch sparked the Space Race. You'll wonder how the astronauts squeezed into space capsules when you see the Mercury, Gemini, and Apollo ships.

Before astronauts and cosmonauts flew, research showed how to keep humans alive at high altitudes. The X-Plane artifacts explain that story.

Take in an interactive show in Dr. Goddard's Lab while learning about rocketry principles.

1100 N. Plum St., Hutchinson, KS 67501, (800) 397-0330, cosmo.org

---

TIP

Clyde W. Tombaugh from Burdett discovered Pluto. In his honor, survey the Solar System at Burdett's Rediscover Pluto Miniature Golf Course.

490 345th Ave., Burdett, KS 67523, (620) 525-6279
burdettks.org/index.php?pageID=17459_2

SOAR INTO THE SKIES
AT THE KANSAS AVIATION MUSEUM

Clyde Cessna started a trend. He moved to Wichita in 1916—and helped to turn Wichita into the Air Capital of the World. After Cessna's arrival, airplane manufacturing's most prominent names came to Wichita: Beechcraft, Boeing, Curtiss-Wright, Learjet, and Stearman.

The Kansas Aviation Museum now inhabits the former Wichita Municipal Airport terminal building, an Art Deco treasure. Inside, meet the Kansas Aviation Hall of Fame members, learn about renowned Wichita-based aviation companies, and admire small planes. Examine bigger airplanes on the tarmac outside.

Sit in air traffic controllers' seats in the air traffic control tower. The view offers an excellent panoramic view of Wichita.

Let the kids play around with aviation in the playroom or curl up with an aviation book in the library.

3350 S. George Washington Blvd., Wichita, KS 67210, (316) 683-9242
kansasaviationmuseum.org

TIP

Wichita built 1,644 B-29 Superfortresses during World War II. One of them, Doc, came home to the B-29 Doc Hangar, Education & Visitors Center.

1788 S. Airport Rd., Wichita, KS 67209
(316) 260-4312, b29doc.com

CONQUER THE SKIES WITH KANSAS AVIATION

B-29 Memorial Plaza
Great Bend Municipal Airport
9047 Sixth St., Great Bend, KS 67530
(620) 793-5125, b29memorial.com

Chanute-Wright Brothers Memorial
Honors flight pioneers Octave Chanute and Orville
and Wilbur Wright
5 W. Main St., Chanute, KS 66720, (620) 431-3350
discoverchanute.com

Clarence Audburn Gilbert Memorial
First airmail pilot to lose his life during a night flight
Plainville Post Office, 111 S. Main St., Plainville, KS 67663
getruralkansas.org/Plainville/119Explore/468.shtml

Combat Air Museum
Forbes Field, 7016 SE Forbes Ave., Topeka, KS 66619
(785) 862-3303, combatairmuseum.org

Emil W. Roesky, Jr., Memorial
Aviation Heritage Museum
Pfister Park, N. Cline Rd., Coffeyville, KS 67337
(620) 251-2550
coffeyville.com/314/Aviation-Heritage-Museum

Exploration Place
Interactive aviation exhibit
300 N. McLean Blvd., Wichita, KS 67203
(316) 660-0600, exploration.org

High Plains Museum
America's First Patented Helicopter
1717 Cherry Ave., Goodland, KS 67735
(785) 890-4595, highplainsmuseum.org

Mid-America Air Museum
2000 W. Second St., Liberal, KS 67901, (620) 624-5263
cityofliberal.org/191/Mid-America-Air-Museum

TANGLE WITH TORNADOES
FOR THREE STRAIGHT YEARS IN CODELL

Codell residents needed coats on the morning of May 20, 1918. Based on past experience, they reasoned that cool weather did not spawn tornadoes; only sultry weather brought vicious vortices. They hoped the low temperatures would end their unlucky tornado streak.

They were disappointed.

The May 20, 1916, F2 tornado and the May 20, 1917, F3 tornado had only destroyed property. Both had arrived in the afternoon.

On May 20, 1918, the funnel cloud did not descend until 8 p.m. The F4 tornado killed 10 people and injured dozens. It also leveled most of Codell's business district, and many businesses never reopened. Codell's economy has never recovered.

The cruel twister streak ended in 1918.

On the 1918 tornado's centennial, the community dedicated a memorial, a 12-foot tall stylized tornado.

303 Fourth St., Codell, KS 67663, (785) 425-6881, rookscounty.net/attractions

---

TIP

On May 4, 2007, an EF5 tornado destroyed 95 percent of Greensburg. The Big Well Museum preserves artifacts from the day Greensburg nearly disappeared.

315 S. Sycamore St., Greensburg, KS 67054
(620) 723-4102, bigwell.org

STAND IN THE CENTER
AT THE GEOGRAPHIC CENTER
OF THE LOWER 48 STATES

Before Alaska and Hawaii joined the Union, a government scientist cut out a cardboard US map and balanced it on a pencil point to find the Geographic Center of the US. The pencil landed northeast of Lebanon. Supposedly, the pencil pointed to a hog pen, but the local Hub Club wasn't going to send people to a hog pen.

Instead, the club created a small park around a flag-topped cairn. The state paved a short highway to the site. Eat a picnic lunch in the shelter. The park also includes a tiny chapel.

Of course, once the 49th and 50th states came in, Lebanon was no longer the center of the nation, but it still is in the center of the contiguous states.

Hwy. 191, Lebanon, KS 66952, (785) 282-5110
smithcoks.com/VisitorTourismInformationSite/
Lebanon/tabid/13983/Default.aspx

TIP

A replica of the North American Geodetic Center's marker stands in a park at Apollo Ave. and W. 80th Dr., Osborne, KS 67473. While in Osborne, look for the face on the courthouse's south side at 423 W. Main St.

(785) 346-5611, discoverosborne.com

MINE
THE COAL EXPERIENCE
AT BIG BRUTUS

An orange glow above the trees signals visitors that Big Brutus is nearby. The glow resolves into the top of the behemoth's cab. When visitors arrive at the visitor center, the electric shovel dominates the scene.

Numbers only partially explain the Bucyrus Erie model 1850B's vast size: it stands 160 feet (16 stories) tall and weighs 11 million pounds. Its boom is 150 feet long, and its dipper holds up to 150 tons, enough to fill three railroad cars. In 1962, it cost $6.5 million. The shovel stopped operating in 1974.

Climb to the cab, sit in the driver's seat, and pretend to wield the shovel. Soak in the view.

The visitor center includes mining exhibits and the Little Giant. Outside, explore more machinery. Pack a picnic.

6509 NW 60th St., West Mineral, KS 66782, (620) 827-6177
bigbrutus.org

TIP

In its working life, Big Brutus chewed away the overburden from coal seams. Fish, hike, and camp where Brutus bit the Mined Land Wildlife Area.

511 E. 560th Ave., Pittsburg, KS 66762, (620) 231-3173
ksoutdoors.com/KDWPT-Info/Locations/Wildlife-Areas/Southeast/
Mined-Land

HONOR THOSE WHO EXTRACTED MINERALS

From the 1880s to the 1920s, Kansas mined a third of the nation's bituminous coal. Coal powered the railroads and the kilns that processed lead and zinc for the tri-state mining region of Kansas, Missouri, and Oklahoma.

Crawford County Historical Museum
651 S. Hwy. 69, Pittsburg, KS 66762, (620) 231-1440
crawfordcountymuseum.com

Galena Mining and Historical Museum
Prospectors found the mineral galena, lead ore, on the ground, sparking the Galena Lead Rush. Galena is the state's official mineral.
319 W. Seventh St., Galena, KS 66739
(620) 783-2192, galenamuseum.org

Miners Hall Museum
701 S. Broadway, Franklin, KS 66735, (620) 347-4220
minershallmuseum.com

Little Balkans Festival
Mining attracted Eastern European miners, and the region got the name "Little Balkans." The festival celebrates the area's heritage. Attend events in Pittsburg and Frontenac.
Pittsburg, KS 66762, (620) 231-7561
littlebalkansfestival.com

Miners Memorial at Immigrant Park
106 W. Second St., Pittsburg, KS 66762
(620) 231-4100, minersmemorialpittks.org

PROSPECT FOR AN ADVENTURE WORTH ITS SALT
AT STRATACA, THE UNDERGROUND SALT MUSEUM

Via a six-ton hoist, plunge 650 feet down into a salt mine, a place where the temperature is always 50 degrees. Open your mouth and taste the salt in the air, deposited by an ancient sea. You may think of salt as mundane and practical. But once you see the glinting crystals in the Permian Room's walls, you'll change your mind.

Salt is beautiful—and essential. The mine opened in 1923, and it's still going. Customers use Hutchinson Salt Co.'s products for construction, livestock feed, snow removal, and weed killing.

Strataca guests ride mine trains through tunnels while learning about geology and the daily work of miners.

The UV&S Gallery is the highlight of the tour. UV&S specializes in secure storage, and some of their movie items are on display.

3650 E. Ave. G, Hutchinson, KS 67501, (620) 662-1425, underkansas.org

---

TIP
In 1887, Ben Blanchard was searching for oil but found salt instead. View the Salt Discovery Well.

1 Discovery Loop, South Hutchinson, KS 67505, (620) 663-7104
southhutch.com/804/Attractions

TURN BACK THE CLOCK
AT SHAWNEE TOWN 1929

The world was a different place in 1929. Electricity, running water, sewers, and telephone services were in their infancy, and many families lacked them. Hand- or muscle-powered machines accomplished most tasks.

Shawnee Town 1929 offers opportunities to re-enter that world as a Shawnee truck farmer or small-town businessperson.

Back then, people grew their own vegetables, made their own soap for washing clothes on a washboard, milked cows, churned butter, fed the chickens, and gathered their eggs. Time travelers can join in the chores.

Prohibition was in full swing in Kansas, but the citizens often ignored it. "Evade" the law in the speakeasy-style wedding venue.

For a touch of the macabre, examine the museum's undertaker's collection. Witness how the business of death has evolved.

11501 W. 57th St., Shawnee, KS 66203, (913) 248-2360
shawneetown.org

TIP
Kick off summer fun at the annual Old Shawnee Days festival, including one of the state's largest parades.

oldshawneedays.org

ENCOUNTER THE KUSKA COLLECTION
AT THE PRAIRIE MUSEUM
OF ART & HISTORY

Colby's Nellie Kuska was an avid collector—so avid that she and her husband, Joe, had enough for a California museum nicknamed "The Smithsonian of the West." When they died, the contents came to Colby in several moving vans stuffed with dolls, glassware, buttons, and numerous other items.

When the Prairie Museum inherited the collection, they needed a home for it. Architect George Kuska, Joe and Nellie's son, designed a concrete building encircled by the earth.

The grasses that wave atop the main building tie it to the museum's outbuildings, including the vast Cooper Barn. When the barn came to Colby, the spectacle attracted huge crowds. The barn now anchors the museum's prairie living site, including a church, a school, a 1930s farmhouse, and a sod house.

1905 S. Franklin Ave., Colby, KS 67701, (785) 460-4590
prairiemuseum.org

TIP

Fifteen minutes to the east in Mingo, search for
the World's Oldest Active Geocache.

geocaching.com/geocache/GC30_mingo

● ●

PONDER THE MYSTERY
OF THE DAVIS MEMORIAL

John Milburn Davis was not Hiawatha's favorite son. His motivations eluded his neighbors.

He and his wife Sarah had lived frugally until she died in 1930. The couple was childless.

After Sarah was gone, John's spending habits changed. He created an elaborate memorial to his wife's "sacred memory." He removed their simple headstone and ordered 11 detailed sculptures.

Hiawatha begged Davis to invest in city projects. He refused. Citizens said Davis created the memorial to prevent Sarah's family from receiving an inheritance. However, Davis was secretly giving aid to poor people.

Davis died in 1947 and rests next to Sarah. Their elaborate memorial draws people to Hiawatha, attracting thousands of visitors annually.

Davis took his reasons for purchasing the monuments to his grave, leaving the "why" question unanswered.

606 Iowa St., Hiawatha, KS 66434, (785) 742-7643
cityofhiawatha.org/visitors/what-to-see-do/davis-memorial

TIP
Pick up a tasty meal at The Bread Bowl Restaurant & Bakery.
100 Oregon St., (785) 288-1480, facebook.com/BreadBowlToGo

ACCESS GRASSROOTS CREATIVITY
IN THE GRASSROOTS ART CAPITAL

The World's Largest Souvenir Plate welcomes visitors to Lucas. The plate alerts guests that they are about to enter no ordinary city. Lucas's quirky attractions started with the surreal Garden of Eden. People flocked to see the garden, and it inspired others.

Need a pit stop? Bowl Plaza is the craziest public restroom you've ever used. Shaped like a giant toilet, it's full of bathroom artwork. The World's Largest Collection of the World's Smallest Versions of the World's Largest Things is down the street.

The Grassroots Arts Center embraces the work of self-taught artists. Tickets also include the Post Rock Limestone Courtyard, the Florence Deeble Rock Garden, and the bizarre Mri-Pilar's House of Isis.

Millers' Park is full of stone houses and "mountains" that Roy and Clara Miller created as trip souvenirs.

Lucas Chamber of Commerce
201 S. Main St., Lucas, KS 67648, (785) 525-6288, lucaskansas.com

---

TIP
Since 1922, Brant's Market has crafted
bologna and sausage using Czech family recipes.

125 S. Main St., (785) 525-6464, brantsmarket.com

DELVE INTO GRASSROOTS ART IN KANSAS

Erie Dinosaur Park
405 E. Fourth St., Erie, KS 66733, (620) 244-3461
facebook.com/dinosaurparkks

The Giant Grasshopper
6740 Commerce Rd., Goodland, KS 67735
roxieontheroad.com/giant-grasshopper

M. T. Liggett Art Environment
W. Hwy. 400, Mullinville, KS 67109
greensburgks.org/visitors/attractions-activities/
m.t.-liggett-art-work

Jim Dickerman's "Open Range Zoo"
Art along Highways 18 and 14
Lucas, Lincoln, Beverly, Tescott, and beyond
livelincolncounty.com/open-range-zoo

Truckhenge
4124 NE Brier Rd., Topeka, KS 66616
(785) 234-3486, visit.topekapartnership.com/blog/
post/theres-no-place-like-truckhenge

World's Largest Ball of Sisal Twine
Call the caretaker to add twine to the ball.
719 Wisconsin St., Cawker City, KS 67430
(785) 781-4470, cawkercitykansas.com/ball-of-twine.html

BURN, BURN, BURN AT THE RING OF FIRE
AROUND *THE KEEPER OF THE PLAINS*

Nearly every night, park personnel light the Ring of Fire around *The Keeper of the Plains*. The fire drums burn for 15 minutes, illuminating the surrounding Big and Little Arkansas Rivers. Watching the fire reflected in the rivers and gleaming on the Keeper is a magical experience. You'll want to repeat it frequently.

Kiowa-Comanche painter and sculptor Blackbear Bosin donated the Keeper to Wichita's citizens in 1974. In 2007, the city mounted the 44-foot sculpture on top of a 30-foot rock promontory. Two pedestrian bridges connect to the Keeper's plaza. The bridges' shapes commemorate bows and arrows.

Sage, bottlebrush, medicinal herbs, prairie grass, yucca, and cacti surround the boulders and fire drums. When the plants are blooming, their scents add to the ambiance.

650 N. Seneca, Wichita, KS 67203, (316) 303-8663
wichita.gov/Arts/Pages/Keeper.aspx

TIP

The Mid-America All-Indian Museum,
next door to the Keeper, preserves indigenous art and culture.

650 N. Seneca, (316) 350-3340, theindiancenter.org

PRESERVE INDIGENOUS PEOPLE'S HERITAGE

Chetopa Historical Museum
Osage Chief Chetopah exhibit
406 Locust St., Chetopa, KS 67336, (620) 236-7121
facebook.com/Chetopa-historical-
museum-870258353056674

Charles Curtis House
First Native American Vice President
1101 Topeka Blvd., Topeka, KS 66612, (785) 357-1371
visit.topekapartnership.com/listing/charles-curtis-
house-museum/109

Haskell Indian Nations University Cultural Center
155 Indian Ave., Lawrence, KS 66046, (785) 832-6686
haskell.edu/cultural-center

Historic Adobe Museum
Petroglyphs and arrowhead collection,
encampment on the Cimarron River
300 E. Oklahoma Ave., Ulysses, KS 67880
(620) 356-3009, grantcoks.org/552/Visit-Our-Museum

Indian Pay Station & Museum
Original pay station where the Pottawatomie Nation
received treaty payments
111 E. Mission St., St. Mary's, KS 66536, (785) 437-6600
smks.info/museum.html

Pawnee Indian Museum State Historic Site
Pawnee earth lodge floor from the late 1700s
480 Pawnee Trail, Republic, KS 66964, (785) 361-2255
kshs.org/pawnee_indian

Shawnee Mission State Historic Site
Manual training school for indigenous children
from 1839 to 1862
3403 W. 53rd St., Fairway, KS 66205, (913) 262-0867
kshs.org/shawnee_indian

UNCOVER THE POLITICAL ROOTS OF THE AMERICAN CIVIL WAR
IN HISTORIC LECOMPTON

In 1856, Kansas Territory elected a legislature to sit at the territorial capital in Lecompton. Even though the election was fraudulent, President Franklin Pierce endorsed it.

In 1855, Free-Staters had held a constitutional convention in Topeka, banning slavery. Pierce denounced Topeka and cleared the way for a Lecompton constitutional convention.

The Lecompton convention created a pro-slavery constitution in September 1857. New president James Buchanan endorsed the Lecompton Constitution.

Buchanan's actions split the Democratic Party. Then Kansans overwhelmingly rejected the Lecompton Constitution. The Democrats' split helped to elect Abraham Lincoln and set the stage for the Civil War.

Visit the Constitution Hall State Historic Site and the Territorial Capital Museum, then stroll through Lecompton on the walking trail. (Dwight Eisenhower's parents, David and Ida, met at Lecompton's Lane University.)

Historic Lecompton, 640 E. Woodson Ave., Lecompton, KS 66050
(785) 887-6148, lecomptonkansas.com

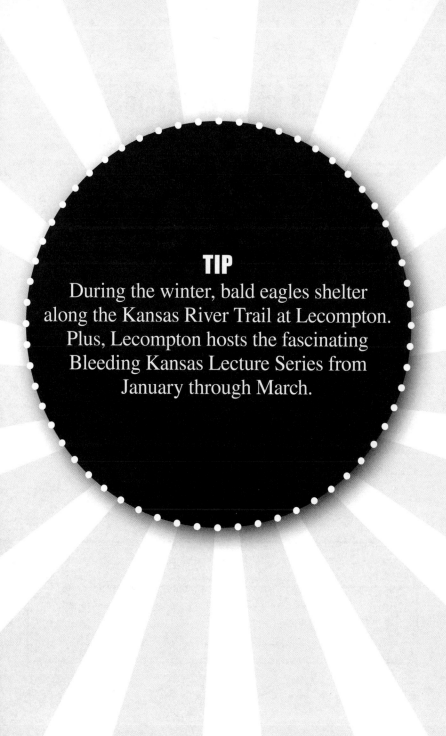

TIP
During the winter, bald eagles shelter along the Kansas River Trail at Lecompton. Plus, Lecompton hosts the fascinating Bleeding Kansas Lecture Series from January through March.

BLEED WITH KANSAS
AT THE JOHN BROWN MUSEUM
STATE HISTORIC SITE

John Brown loathed slavery, and fought several bloody battles against those who were determined to preserve it. Among the most famous of the battles was in Osawatomie.

Some pro-slavery settlers from Georgia had moved near Osawatomie. On August 7, 1856, Brown and others attacked the settlers and burned down their homes.

Three weeks later, Brown and approximately 30 others battled about 250 pro-slavery men in the Battle of Osawatomie. The slavers intended to destroy the town. Brown and his men retreated to a stone corral and shot at the slavers until they ran out of ammunition. They fled to draw away the slavers from Osawatomie. Instead, the slavers plundered the town. Six free-staters, including John's son Frederick, and two pro-slavery men died.

10th and Main Sts., Osawatomie, KS 66064, (913) 755-4384
kshs.org/p/john-brown-museum/19574

TIP

Visit several more John Brown-related sites in Osawatomie: John Brown Park, the Old Stone Church, the Osawatomie Museum, and the Soldiers' Monument.

osawatomieks.org/category/history

WHEN KANSAS BLED: BLEEDING KANSAS AND THE CIVIL WAR

The Battle of Black Jack
Brown's first battle against slavery, effectively the
first battle of the Civil War
163 E. 2000 Rd., Wellsville, KS 66092, (785) 883-2106
blackjackbattlefield.org/the-battle-of-black-jack.html

Baxter Springs Heritage Center and Museum
Exhibit about the 1863 Battle of Fort Blair
740 East Ave., Baxter Springs, KS 66713, (620) 856-2385
baxterspringsmuseum.org

Constitution Hall and Old State Capitol
The first free-state capitol
429 S. Kansas Ave., Ste. 427, Topeka, KS 66603, (785) 250-8228
oldkansascapitol.org

The First Territorial Capitol State Historic Site
693 Huebner Rd., Fort Riley, KS 66442, (785) 238-2422
kshs.org/p/first-territorial-capitol/19572

Marais des Cygnes Massacre State Historic Site
In 1858, pro-slavery men murdered 11 free-state men.
26426 E. 1700th Rd., Pleasanton, KS 66075, (913) 352-8890
kshs.org/marais

Mine Creek Battlefield State Historic Site
1864 Civil War battlefield
20485 Hwy. 52, Pleasanton, KS 66075, (913) 352-8890
kshs.org/p/mine-creek-civil-war-battlefield/19567

Watkins Museum of History
Exhibits cover the Sacking of Lawrence and Quantrill's Raid.
1047 Massachusetts St., Lawrence, KS 66044
(785) 841-4109, watkinsmuseum.org

STRIDE LIKE JOHN BROWN
AT THE KANSAS STATE CAPITOL

In the Kansas State Capitol mural *Tragic Prelude*, John Brown strides through the land like an avenger, a Bible in one hand and a rifle in the other. Tribulations of weather, prairie fires, and civil war follow him.

Vocal opponents blocked the mural artist John Steuart Curry's plans. Frustrated, he abandoned the project. He refused to sign the murals and left his home state forever. In 2015, Kansas inducted him into the capitol's Kansas Walk of Honor.

Topeka's rock band Kansas used the mural for its debut album cover.

The capitol also features Construction Hall, the Notable Kansans exhibit, the Hall of Native Peoples, the first 34-star flag, and events that changed Kansas and the nation. In the Capitol Store, buy Capitol Copper jewelry made from the former roof.

300 W. 10th Ave., Topeka, KS 66612, (785) 296-3966
kshs.org/capitol

TIP
Climb the 296 steps to the top of the dome for breathtaking views.
kshs.org/p/kansas-state-capitol-dome-tours/18467

REFLECT
AT THE BROWN V. BOARD OF EDUCATION NATIONAL HISTORIC SITE

The Rev. Oliver Brown held his third-grade daughter Linda Brown's hand as they walked to all-white Sumner Elementary School in 1951. But the principal said that because the Browns were black, Linda would have to attend Monroe Elementary School across Topeka.

The Browns and others sued the Topeka Board of Education. On May 17, 1954, the Supreme Court struck down segregation as inherently unequal.

Linda never attended Sumner because she was in an integrated junior high when the Supreme Court issued their ruling on Brown v. Board.

In 2004, Monroe Elementary opened as the Brown v. Board of Education National Historic Site. The national historic site has restored the Monroe kindergarten room to its 1950s appearance.

1515 SE Monroe St., Topeka, KS 66612, (785) 354-4273, nps.gov/brvb

---

TIP

Step across the street from the national historic site to view the *Brown v. Board of Education* mural at 1515 SE Monroe Street. visit.topekapartnership.com/things-to-do/the-crossroads-to-freedom/ african-american-history/african-american-murals

CELEBRATE CIVIL RIGHTS
AT THE KANSAS AFRICAN-AMERICAN MUSEUM

For her role as Mammy in *Gone with the Wind*, Hattie McDaniel became the first African-American actor to win an Academy Award. She was born in Wichita. The Kansas African-American Museum (TKAAM) inducted McDaniel into the Trailblazer Hall of Fame in 2020. In 2021, the museum cooperated with others to install a commemorative marker at McDaniel's childhood home, 925 N. Wichita Street.

Like McDaniel's birthplace, TKAAM's home, the former Calvary Baptist Church, had to fight for its place in the sun. When the church moved, Doris Kerr Larkins organized a group to save the building and found a Kansas African-American historical society. Eventually, the group became the TKAAM.

TKAAM explains the African-American experience in Kansas and showcases a fascinating African art collection.

601 N. Water St., Wichita, KS 67203, (316) 262-7651
tkaamuseum.org

TIP

The Kansas City Monarchs minor-league baseball team's name pays tribute to the Negro Leagues' longest-running franchise.

Legends Field, 1800 Village West Pkwy., Kansas City, KS 66111
(913) 328-5618, monarchsbaseball.com

NEVER GIVE UP ON FREEDOM: KANSAS AFRICAN-AMERICAN HISTORY

George Washington Carver sites
Ottawa County Historical Museum
110 S. Concord St., Minneapolis, KS 67467, (785) 392-3621
Historical marker
W. Hwy. 96, Beeler, KS 67518, (785) 798-2413
kansassampler.org/8wondersofkansas-people/george-washington-carver-minneapolis-beeler

Dockum Sit-In Sculpture
First sit-in to integrate restaurants
Chester I. Lewis Reflection Square Park
104 S. Broadway, Wichita, KS 67202
wichita.gov/ParkandRec/CityParks/Pages/ReflectionSquare.aspx

Gordon Parks Museum
Internationally known photographer,
writer, filmmaker, and musician
Fort Scott Community College
2108 S. Horton St., Fort Scott, KS 66701, (620) 223-2700
gordonparkscenter.org

Mount Mitchell Heritage Prairie
Westernmost Underground Railroad route
29377 Mitchell Prairie Ln., Wamego, KS 66547
(785) 221-4061, mountmitchellprairie.org

Nicodemus National Historic Site
Black settlers called Exodusters fled Jim Crow laws.
304 Washington Ave., Nicodemus, KS 67625
(785) 839-4233, nps.gov/nico

The Richard Allen Cultural Center and Museum
Buffalo Soldier's home: artifacts include bust of Cathay
Williams, the only known female Buffalo Soldier.
412 Kiowa St., Leavenworth, KS 66048, (913) 682-8772
jazzbytheriverleavenworth.com/museum

IMMERSE YOURSELF IN FRONTIER LIFE
AT THE MAHAFFIE STAGE STOP & FARM

In 1821, William Becknell successfully reached Santa Fe, New Mexico, blazing the 800-mile Santa Fe Trail. The Mexicans had overthrown the Spanish government and were eager to trade. Becknell nearly died on the trip, but his hard-won knowledge enabled him to map the trail for others.

Imagine the lines of wagons creaking for long, weary miles across the dusty plains.

The Mahaffie Stage Stop & Farm Historic Site in Olathe is the trail's remaining working stage stop. The Mahaffies served 50 to 100 meals daily to stagecoach passengers in their basement. The Westport Route carried traffic from the Santa Fe, Oregon, and California trails.

The historic site offers stagecoach rides, farming, cookstove, and blacksmith demonstrations. Videos tell the Mahaffies' story and discuss Bleeding Kansas and the Civil War.

1200 E. Kansas City Rd., Olathe, KS 66061, (913) 971-5111
mahaffie.org

TIP
Learn about Civil War-era agriculture in the Mahaffie's Agriculture Heritage Barn.

TRADE WITH NEW MEXICO ON THE SANTA FE TRAIL

Council Grove Visitor Center
In 1825, Osage chiefs and federal commissioners
signed a treaty that established the Santa Fe Trail's
right-of-way under the Council Oak.
207 W. Main St., Council Grove, KS 66846
(620) 767-5413, councilgrove.com/chamberandtourism

Flint Hills Trail State Park
The bike trail follows the Santa Fe Trail for 117 miles.
kanzatrails.org/flint-hills-nature-trail

Fort Larned National Historic Site
Fort Larned's troops patrolled 140 miles of the trail.
1767 Hwy. 156, Larned, KS 67550, (620) 285-6911
nps.gov/fols

Lanesfield School Historic Site
Battle of Bull Creek site and a
Santa Fe Trail post office
18745 Dillie Rd., Edgerton, KS 66021, (913) 438-7275
jcprd.com/435/Lanesfield-Historic-Site

Pawnee Rock State Historic Site
The trail's halfway point
SW 112th Ave., Pawnee Rock, KS 67567
(785) 272-8681, ext. 211, kshs.org/pawnee_rock

Point of Rocks
Rock formation signaled nearby natural springs
on the Dry Route.
Hwy. 27 and Rd. 51, Elkhart, KS 67950
geokansas.ku.edu/point-of-rocks

Santa Fe Trail Ruts
One of the best-preserved trail rut sections
Nine miles west of Dodge City on Highway 50
(620) 227-8188, visitdodgecity.org/89/Santa-Fe-Trail

EXPLORE AND DEFEND THE FRONTIER
AT FORT LEAVENWORTH

Meriwether Lewis and William Clark led the Corps of Discovery past the future site of Fort Leavenworth on their epic journey to the Pacific. After the Corps of Discovery's odyssey, the army continued to map and patrol the West until Gen. John J. Pershing pursued Mexican revolutionary Francisco "Pancho" Villa in 1916 and 17. The Frontier Army Museum has collected more than 6,000 artifacts to explain army explorers' adventures.

The Lewis and Clark Center is the headquarters of the Command and General Staff College. The center includes a presidential portrait gallery, two halls of fame, ancient uniforms and artifacts, and stained-glass windows depicting military and patriotic scenes.

For further exploration, the fort's Wayside Tour shows 22 points of interest.

Follow the fort's guest access procedures: home.army.mil/leavenworth/index.php/my-fort/all-services/gate-information.

1 Sherman Ave., Fort Leavenworth, KS 66027, (913) 684-3600
visitleavenworthks.com/visitors/page/fort-leavenworth

● ●

TIP
The Buffalo Soldier Monument
honors the "Buffalo Soldiers,"
the first all-Black regular military unit,
formed at Fort Leavenworth in 1866.

290 Stimson Ave.
Fort Leavenworth, KS 66027, (913) 758-2948
visitleavenworthks.com/visitors/page/
buffalo-soldier-monument

CHARGE INTO HISTORY
AT FORT RILEY

The army's First Infantry Division, the Big Red One, lives at Fort Riley. The army established the division in 1917 for service on World War I's Western Front. Ever since, the Big Red One usually has been the first American division to go to war. Learn about the division's history from its activation until current times at the First Infantry Division Museum.

Before the Big Red One's activation, Fort Riley housed the United States Cavalry School. The all-Black 9th and 10th Cavalry Regiments, "Buffalo Soldiers," were stationed there at various times. The Cavalry Museum tells the cavalry's story from the Revolutionary War until the horse soldiers' demise in the 1950s. The Custer House shows officer's quarters from the 1870s to the 1880s.

Read the fort's visitor access information before you go: home.army.mil/riley/index.php/about/visitor-info.

885 Henry Dr., Marshall Army Airfield, Fort Riley, KS 66442
(785) 239-2982, fortrileyhistoricalsociety.org

TIP
Visit the memorials and attend events in Heritage Park.

Sixth and Washington Sts., Junction City, KS 66441, (785) 238-3103
junctioncity.org/99/Heritage-Park

COMPOSE A SONG FOR UNSUNG HEROES
AT THE LOWELL MILKEN CENTER

Five students in a Uniontown High social studies class read about Irena Sendler, a Polish social worker who saved 2,500 children from the Holocaust. She placed a coded list of the rescued children's real names in jars and buried the jars beneath a tree. At the war's end, the list enabled families to reunite. However, most of the families had died in concentration camps.

Sendler's story is only one of the stories at the Lowell Milken Center for Unsung Heroes. The stories are incredibly moving; you'll need a tissue.

Hear the songs of these heroes: when nine Black students, the Little Rock Nine, integrated Little Rock Central High, only two White students befriended them, Ken Rheinhardt and Ann Williams. To protest racism, Ralph Lazo volunteered to live in a World War II Japanese internment camp. Helen Taussig battled sexism and pioneered pediatric cardiology.

1 S. Main St., Fort Scott, KS 66701
(620) 223-1312, lowellmilkencenter.org

TIP
Fort Scott's soldiers became agents of
America's largest expansion. Visit Fort Scott National Historic Site.

199 Old Fort Blvd., Fort Scott, KS 66701
(620) 223-0310, nps.gov/fosc

FIND A HOME FOR CHILDREN
AT THE NATIONAL ORPHAN TRAIN COMPLEX

At the turn of the last century, impoverished children lived dangerous lives in East Coast cities. No foster care system existed, and charities devised the orphan train movement to rescue children from the streets.

They sent them west. Over 75 years, the movement placed about 250,000 children. Over 2 million descendants came from the orphan train riders.

Not all of the placements were successful, but the placement agents tried to ease the children's lives. Agents visited each child—without others present—twice in their first placement year. The agents returned annually and required annual reports from the foster families.

Concordia's National Orphan Train Complex preserves the movement's history. The vintage railroad passenger car gives a sense of the experiences of the children and their chaperones.

300 Washington St., Concordia, KS 66901, (785) 243-4471
orphantraindepot.org

TIP

Another group, German prisoners of war, debarked from trains in Concordia. See how they fared at the Camp Concordia POW Camp.

1550 Union Rd., Concordia, KS 66901, (785) 243-4303, powcampconcordia.org

Dala horses at Hemslöjd Swedish Gifts

SHOPPING AND FASHION

TRAVEL TO SWEDEN WITH NO PASSPORT
IN LITTLE SWEDEN USA

During his 1976 visit, Swedish King Carl XVI Gustaf said that Lindsborg, Little Sweden USA, is more Swedish than Sweden. But you don't need to be a Swede to cherish Lindsborg. Start at the Swedish Pavilion, Sweden's entry in the 1904 Louisiana Purchase Exposition in St. Louis, and then follow the trail of the Wild Dala Herd.

Walk the Välkommen Trail. (*Välkommen* means "welcome" in Swedish.) Eat at the Crown & Rye, the Öl' Stuga, and Blacksmith Coffee Shop & Roastery. Bring home Swedish ingredients from White's Foodliner.

Start shopping at the Hemslöjd Swedish Gifts. Rent a quadricycle there and pedal it throughout Lindsborg. You'll love downtown Lindsborg's shops, like the Small World Gallery, Trollslända Toy Store, The Good Merchant, Rendezvous Adventure Outfitters, and the White Peacock Tea and Coffee Company.

104 Lincoln St., Lindsborg, KS 67456, (785) 227-8687
visitlindsborg.com

TIP

Enjoy panoramic views of the Smoky Hill Valley at Coronado Heights north of Lindsborg. Arrive at sunrise and eat a picnic breakfast in the castle at the top.

SHOP TO YOUR HEART'S DELIGHT
AT LEGENDS OUTLETS

Legends Outlets combines shopping, eating, drinking, and history for a thoroughly enjoyable experience. Explore more than 100 stores, eateries, and entertainment venues in Kansas City's Village West.

Sporting KC's stadium and the Kansas Speedway are just down the road. Before you go, buy fan gear at Sportibles.

The shopping center has dedicated each of its corridors to a famous Kansan or state aspect. Find Dwight Eisenhower's five stars and his favorite fishing hole. Amelia Earhart's Lockheed Electra is ready to whisk her around the world.

Outlets include the Banana Republic, Brooks Brothers, The Gap, Haggar, Levi's, Old Navy, Chico's, Lane Bryant, F21 Red, Polo Ralph Lauren, Helzburg Diamonds, Converse, and Nike.

Eat at Culver's, Yard House, or Jazz, a Louisiana Kitchen.

1843 Village West Pkwy., Kansas City, KS 66111, (913) 788-3700
legendsshopping.com

TIP
Minutes from Legends, every room
at Chateau Avalon has a theme—and a hot tub.
701 Village West Pkwy., (913) 596-6000, chateauavalonhotel.com

PICK UP
ALL THE MARBLES
AT MOON MARBLE COMPANY

Bruce Breslow had sold wooden toys and games for years, but had difficulty finding quality marbles for them. He envisioned using the marbles he had treasured as a child, varieties like bumblebees, Cub Scouts, puries, and so forth for his games. To fix the problem, he opened the Moon Marble Company.

The store has machine-made marbles in numerous colors, designs, and sizes, from half-inch pee-wee to two-inch toe breakers. Traditional toys, games, retro reproductions, and gifts complete the store's selections.

But the Moon is more than a store. Breslow's marble-making demonstrations are the Moon's highlight. During his demonstrations, he explains glasswork and marble history and tells fascinating stories about marbles. After watching Breslow's magic, look for other prominent glassworkers' creations within the store.

600 E. Front St., Bonner Springs, KS 66012, (913) 441-1432
moonmarble.com

TIP

Every March, the Moon hosts Marble Crazy, a glassworking show. Artists from across the nation demonstrate marble-making techniques for two days.

marblecrazy.com

LIVE IN A SHOPPING AND ENTERTAINMENT MECCA
IN OLD TOWN WICHITA

Converted brick warehouses comprise Old Town Wichita, where you'll never need to leave. Whatever you need is ready for you.

Reserve a room at the Hotel at Old Town in the former Keen Kutter Warehouse. Or rent a loft. Be warned: you may never want to leave.

Dine on a churrasco steak at Sabor Latin Bar & Grille, lamb T-bones at Larkspur, or a Sexy Roll at Blue Fin Sake Bar & Sushi. Raise a glass at Nortons Brewing Company, PourHouseICT, or River City Brewing Co.

Save the planet with Uniquities' unique pieces. Next, shop at Mr. Diggs Dwelling & Co. Escape cookie-cutter fashions at Lucinda's, plus rock Wichita gear.

Enter a time portal at the Museum of World Treasures and the Great Plains Transportation Museum. You may never come out, and that's OK.

Douglas Ave. & Washington, Wichita, KS 67202, oldtownwichita.com

---

TIP
Wichita Farm & Art Market opens every Saturday all year.

835 E. First St., Wichita, KS 67202, (316) 337-5770
oldtownfarmandartmarket.com

COWBOY UP
WITH THE MYSTERY
OF THE COWBOY BOOT'S INVENTOR

Mystery shrouds the cowboy boot's inventor. The first cowboy boot may be from Abilene, Coffeyville, Olathe, or (God forbid) somewhere in Texas.

Legend says that an unnamed cowboy dismounted in front of Charles H. Hyer's Olathe shoe shop in 1875. He ordered new boots with a tall shank, a pointed toe, and a high, slanted heel. Hyer filled the order, and the pleased cowboy spread the word. Hyer had invented the cowboy boot. Eventually, Hyer's store became the Olathe Boot Co.

However, in 1874, T. C. McInerney in Abilene was advertising cowboy boots, and John Cubine was making boots in Chetopa. Two years later, Cubine moved to Coffeyville. His Coffeyville-style boots combined US Cavalry boots with British Wellington boots.

So who invented the cowboy boot? No one knows.

kshs.org/publicat/history/1995spring_brackman.pdf

COWBOY UP AT KANSAS'S TOP WESTERN STORES

Bluboots Western + Work
401 W. Eighth St., Coffeyville, KS 67337
(620) 688-6502, facebook.com/blubootsks

Crazy House
3502 N. Campus Rd., Garden City, KS 67846
(620) 275-1417
702 E. Pancake Blvd., Liberal, KS 67901, (620) 624-0400
crazyhouse.com

El Amigo Western Wear
Towne West Square, 4600 W. Kellogg Dr., Wichita, KS
67209, (316) 946-0155, facebook.com/AmigoWW

Las Trancas Western Wear
2445 S. Seneca St., Wichita, KS 67217, (316) 305-5337
facebook.com/LasTrancasWesternWear

Nigro's Western Store
3320 Merriam Ln., Kansas City, KS 66106,
(913) 262-7500
10509 Shawnee Mission Pkwy., Shawnee, KS 66203
(913) 631-2226
nigroswesternstore.com

The Outpost Western Store
7003 Tuttle Creek Blvd., Manhattan, KS 66503
(785) 539-7316, outpostboots.com

Rittel's Western Wear
Home of the former World's Largest Spur
1810 N. Buckeye Ave., Abilene, KS 67410
(785) 263-1800, rittelswesternwearllc.com

S&S Western Outfitters
101 Delaware St., Edna, KS 67342, (620) 922-3613
sandslumberandmetalsales.com/ss-western-outfitters

Yee Haw Country Outfitters
431 Poyntz Ave., Manhattan, KS 66502, (785) 320-2570
yeehawmhk.com

OBTAIN YOUR DESIRES
AT OAK PARK MALL

Oak Park Mall sprawls over 1.5 million square feet. The shopping mecca is both Kansas's most extensive and Kansas City's largest indoor mall.

Dillard's, Nordstrom, Macy's, and JCPenney anchor the mall. Dozens more retailers fill the remaining two levels of stores. Choose from more than 20 food options in the food court. Decide whether On the Border, Chick-Fil-A, Bibibop Asian Grill, or Nestlé Toll House Café fits your mood.

Aldo, Coach, Sephora, Francesca's, Garage, Perfume Galaxy, Zumiez, Hot Topic, Windsor, and Jewelry Doctors are waiting for you.

Are you shopping with kids? Take them to Build-a-Bear, LEGO, and Go! Calendars, Games & Toys.

Adopt a kitty at Purrfect Pets Cat Adoptions.

Don't worry about parking. There are plenty of spaces available.

11149 W. 95th St., Overland Park, KS 66214, (913) 888-4400
thenewoakparkmall.com

TIP
Before you start shopping, check the mall's deals page.
thenewoakparkmall.com/deals

ADORN YOURSELF WITH STYLE
ON MASS STREET

Downtown Lawrence is Lawrence's heart, and Massachusetts Street is the heart of downtown. Call it Mass Street for short.

Style your home and your body at KB & Co.'s six boutiques. Set clothing trends at Swanson's. Support your favorite team with gear from Rally House/Kansas Sampler and Jock's Nitch. Weaver's has exclusive Jayhawk products. Prepare for outdoor fun at Sunflower Outdoor & Bike Shop. Bring your pet a gift from Lucky Dog Outfitters.

Groove to the music with CDs and records at Love Garden Sounds. Create music with Mass Street Music's instruments. Curl up with a good book at the Raven Book Store.

Shopping makes you hungry. Satisfy your cravings at Wheatfields Bakery & Café, the Mad Greek Restaurant, Mass Street Soda, The Roost, and Torched Goodness Food Truck.

Downtown Lawrence, Inc.
833 1/2 Massachusetts St., Lawrence, KS 66044, (785) 842-3883
downtownlawrence.com

TIP
Celebrate Lawrence during downtown Lawrence's events.

downtownlawrence.com/events

SAVOR DINING AND SHOPPING
IN DOWNTOWN HAYS

Downtown Hays bustles with shoppers and diners strolling on its brick streets. Fill your to-visit list with 44 restaurants and shops, 15 arts and historic sites, and 14 entertainment venues.

For dining, start with Tiger Burgers, Gella's Diner, Sake2Me Sushi & Seafood Grille, or the Paisley Pear.

Shop at The Bluetique, Madd Matter Frame Shop & Gallery, Couture for Men, Be Made, and Refine.

The Hays Arts Council is the state's oldest. Admire sculptures at Pete Felten's Stone Gallery.

Early Hays was wild—wild enough to start the West's first Boot Hill Cemetery. People with near-mythical reputations walked its streets: George Armstrong Custer, Mary Jane "Calamity Jane" Cannary, William F. "Buffalo Bill" Cody, and James Butler "Wild Bill" Hickok. Twenty-seven bronze plaques tell early Hays stories.

Downtown Hays Development Corporation
1200 Main St., Ste. 102, Hays, KS 67601, (785) 621-4171
downtownhays.com

TIP
Hang out during the shopping district's events.
downtownhays.com/events-calendar

MELT AWAY STRESS
AT THE PRAIRIE LAVENDER FARM

The aroma of fresh lavender wafts through the air during the blooming season at Prairie Lavender Farm. You feel yourself relaxing, and it's not your imagination. As you walk around the farm, the rows of lavender wrap around you, calming and soothing you. The rows contain 4,600 plants divided between 12 varieties of lavender.

Aromatherapists use lavender to ease headaches, nervousness, and sleeplessness. Lavender also soothes acne, eczema, diaper rash, and sunburns. It calms upset stomachs.

Take home the wonderful lavender feeling. Prairie Lavender Farm creates a range of naturally-made products with their lavender. Their line includes essential oils, a headache relief stick, lavender tea blends, soap, bath salts, wreaths, and lavender lovers' gift boxes.

69 Alpine Ridge Ln., Bennington, KS 67422, (785) 488-3371
prairielavenderfarm.com

TIP
Visit the farm during their annual plant sale,
lavender festival, and other events.

TAKE KANSAS HOME
AT KANSAS ORIGINALS
MARKET & GALLERY

Kansas Originals is a Kansas-themed shopping destination. Kansas authors, photographers, painters, crafters, and food producers fill the store. A jury has approved every item to ensure that everything is worth buying.

Every souvenir store offers T-shirts, but this store's selection is exceptional. Buy Post Rock signs, picture frames, and desk sets. Sculptors carve wooden miniatures and create larger works in copper, brass, and iron. Remember the Sunflower State with sunflower ceramics. Potters impress their products with wheat and leaves.

Choose photographs or drawings of Kansas landscapes.

Adorn yourself or a loved one with Kansas jewelry and clothing.

Taste Kansas with salsas, barbecue sauces, jams, and jellies. Add dip mixes and buffalo sausage, and buy popcorn and fudge for a snack.

Look for the room with the free travel guides.

233 Hwy. 232, Wilson, KS 67490, (785) 658-2602
kansasoriginals.com

TIP
Look for another Kansas Originals shop
on the Kansas Turnpike, five miles east of Topeka.

RELIVE THE WILD WEST
AT THE JERRY THOMAS GALLERY & COLLECTION

Enter artist Jerry Thomas's fascinating world at the Jerry Thomas Gallery & Collection in Scott City. Thomas is well-known for creating detailed, realistic, and meticulously researched images of animals and Western history.

Thomas's artwork fills the gallery. As you walk through, you'll understand his popularity. The prints are stunning. Famous warriors and soldiers come to life as you examine the paintings. The animals seem to leap off the wall.

Besides his artwork, the gallery includes Thomas's extensive historical artifact collection. Near Scott City, soldiers fought Northern Cheyennes at the Battle of Punished Woman's Fork, the US Army's final battle in Kansas. Lt. Col. William H. Lewis died from a gunshot wound; he was the last soldier killed in Kansas. Thomas's collection includes Lewis's sword and the only known picture of him.

902 W. Hwy. 96, Scott City, KS 67871, (785) 410-6667
jerrythomasartgallery.com

TIP
The gallery shares a building with the El Quartelejo Museum.
(620) 872-5912, elquartelejomuseum.org

PURCHASE THE PERFECT ANTIQUE
IN WINFIELD'S ANTIQUE STORES

Seven antique stores within six blocks make Winfield a prime destination for antique hunters. Browse the stores' inventories and picture how you could use the items on display.

The Emporium requires its dealers to offer 60 percent antiques in their booths.

Junk Generation specializes in primitives and windows.

The Funky Junky Girls repurpose vintage items.

Trunk N' Treasures is full of consignment items from more than 40 vendors.

Grit and Glitter carry home décor, signs, refurbished furniture, and vintage gifts.

Virginia Jarvis Antiques' showroom spreads over 6,000 square feet. If you don't know what to buy your special someone, let the store's shopping service help you.

cca.winfieldchamber.org/Tourism-Retail-Antiques-__8304_membergroup.aspx

---

TIP

Between stores, eat at Shindig's Bar & Grill.

500 Main St., Winfield, KS 67156, (620) 221-4782
shindigsbarandgrill.com

SEEK A CHIC ANTIQUE

AnTeaQues
415 Main St., Courtland, KS 66939, (785) 374-9292
anteaques.net

Encore Antiques
590 S. Fossil St., Russell, KS 67665, 785-445-8480
facebook.com/encore.veez

Heirloom Obsessions
142 S. Fifth St., Chetopa, KS 67336, (620) 717-2191
facebook.com/HeirloomObsessions

Junk in the Trunk Emporium
4535 E. 61st St. N, Kechi, KS 67067, (316) 613-8788
facebook.com/junkinthetrunkemporium

Main Street Mercantile
One of five shops on Westmoreland's Antique Row
310 Main St., Westmoreland, KS 66547, (785) 556-1626
themercantiques.com/antiques-row.html

MorMor's Antiques
212 E. 17th St., Goodland, KS 67735, (785) 772-6168
facebook.com/mormorsantiques

Paramount Antique Malls & Marketplace
Paramount has three stores, two in Wichita and one in
Augusta. paramountantiquemall.com

Poehler Mercantile Antique Mall
301 Commercial St., Emporia, KS 66801, (620) 341-9092
facebook.com/poehlerantique

Two Vintage Sisters
1104 S. Denver St., El Dorado, KS 67042, (316) 452-5775
twovintagesisters.net

BUILD YOUR BRAIN
WITH MINDSCULPT GAMES

MindSculpt Games carries a mind-boggling game selection.

Daniel and Darcy Leech dreamed of owning a game store, a natural outgrowth of their hobbies. The former teachers' goals are to build people's minds and strengthen relationships and communities.

MindSculpt is the Leech family's dream come true. It's also a dream come true for game lovers and hobbyists.

Find these items and more at MindSculpt:

A 5,000-square-foot store dedicated to fun. Sports, Magic: the Gathering, and Pokemon cards. Numerous game console brands and video games. Beanie Babies. Card and dice games. Aisles of puzzles and educational games. Star Wars merch. Models. Comic books. Science kits.

Build relationships and community on game nights. Paint, play Warhammer, Dungeons & Dragons, and other role-playing games in the store's game-playing area.

4908 10th St., Great Bend, KS 67530, (620) 603-8462
mindsculptgames.com

TIP
If choosing between 200 board games overwhelms you, rent a game—and get a discount if you decide to purchase it.

● ●

FURNISH YOUR HOME
AT MILLER'S OF CLAFLIN

Miller's of Claflin is vast, with a selection to match. The store spans both sides of a city block, with 13 showrooms spreading over nearly 100,000 feet of floor space. The showrooms hold the most extensive selection of furniture between Kansas City and Denver. Customers arrive from Kansas and surrounding states.

Claflin's entire population could sit in the store's living room sets. More than 70 bedroom sets stock the bedroom department.

As Miller's has expanded, the company has restored Claflin's storefronts to their former appearances.

Cover your home's floors and fill your house with furnishings all in one stop. Don't worry about bringing home your purchases or removing your old furniture. In Kansas, Miller's takes care of delivery and removal—for free.

200 Main St., Claflin, KS 67525, (620) 587-3601
millersofclaflin.com

TIP
The buggy in the first showroom belonged to founder J. W. Miller. The family restored it and hung it from the original pressed-tin ceiling.

FUEL YOUR FIBER ART PASSIONS
AT THE SHEPHERD'S MILL

The Shepherd's Mill manufactures yarn and fabric from a zoo's worth of animals, from alpaca to yak. When raw fiber comes in, the mill begins a multi-stage process to make yarn. More steps end with a woven work of art available in their store. This is the oldest and largest fiber mill in Kansas, and the country's most versatile.

Besides their finished goods, the store sells fiber-making tools and equipment. Are you interested in creating fiber artwork? Take classes at the Mill.

The owners, Jay and Sally Brandon, have deep roots in Phillipsburg. They live on the land his family homesteaded four generations ago.

Sally's fiber root system runs to Finland. During six months living there, she discovered a passion for creating cloth. The love continues at the Mill.

839 Third St., Phillipsburg, KS 67661, (785) 543-3128
kansasfiber.com

TIP

See a terrific model-railroad layout at C&R Railroad Museum, also in Phillipsburg.

860 Park St., Phillipsburg, KS 67661
(785) 543-5535
cityofphillipsburg.com/207/Attractions

Alfalfa field southwest of Norton

SUGGESTED
ITINERARIES

DATE NIGHT

Travel to Sweden with No Passport in Little Sweden USA, 144

Feast on the Extraordinary at The Elephant Bistro & Bar, 18

Ride the Rails on the Kansas Belle Dinner Train, 52

Quaff Liquid Bread at Gella's Diner and Lb. Brewing, 26

Live in a Shopping and Entertainment Mecca in Old Town Wichita, 147

Come Together Right Now at the Historic Stiefel Theatre, 44

Sneak Away to a Vintage Roadhouse at North Star Steakhouse, 16

Scoot Your Boots Below the Bar at Boot Hill Distillery, 25

FOR THE ENTIRE FAMILY

Dine with the Dynasty in the Fried Chicken Capital of Kansas, 10

Grab the Brass Ring at C. W. Parker Carousel Museum, 46

Survive a (Fake) Shoot-out at the Boot Hill Museum, 53

Join the Party at the Christmas City of the High Plains, 55

Roam Where the Buffalo Call Home at Maxwell Wildlife Refuge, 102

Follow the Yellow Brick Road to the Emerald City of Oz, 106

Pick Up All the Marbles at Moon Marble Company, 146

Rock Your World at Little Jerusalem Badlands State Park, 78

Encounter the Kuska Collection at the Prairie Museum of Art & History, 120

• •

DOWN ON THE FARM

UNIQUE AND QUIRKY

BREATHE THE FRESH AIR

A DATE WITH HISTORY

GIRLFRIEND WEEKEND

BECOME AN OVERCOMER

● ●

GAME NIGHT

ACTIVITIES
BY SEASON

SPRING

SUMMER

• •

FALL

WINTER

• •

INDEX

• •

● ●